Summary

Congress periodically establishes agricultural and food policy in an omnibus farm bill. The 112th Congress faces reauthorization of the current five-year farm bill (the Food, Conservation, and Energy Act of 2008, P.L. 110-246) because many of its provisions expire in 2012. The 2008 farm bill contained 15 titles covering farm commodity support, horticulture, livestock, conservation, nutrition assistance, international trade and food aid, agricultural research, farm credit, rural development, bioenergy, and forestry, among others.

The Senate Agriculture Committee approved its version of the 2012 omnibus farm bill on April 26, 2012 (Agriculture Reform, Food, and Jobs Act of 2012), and officially filed the measure, S. 3240, on May 24, 2012. Within its 12 titles, the five-year Senate bill would reshape the structure of farm commodity support, expand crop insurance coverage, consolidate conservation programs, revise the Supplemental Nutrition Assistance Program (formerly food stamps), and extend authority to appropriate funds for many U.S. Department of Agriculture (USDA) discretionary programs through FY2017. Senate floor action on the measure is expected in June, as is House Agriculture Committee consideration of its version of a 2012 farm bill.

I0454956

Contents

Tables

Contacts

Introduction

The 112th Congress is in the midst of considering an omnibus farm bill that will establish the direction of agricultural policy for the next several years. Many provisions of the current farm bill (the Food, Conservation, and Energy Act of 2008, P.L. 110-246) expire this year. The Senate Agriculture Committee approved its version of the 2012 omnibus farm bill on April 26, 2012 (Agriculture Reform, Food and Jobs Act of 2012), and officially filed the measure, S. 3240, on May 24, 2012. Within its 12 titles, the five-year Senate bill would reshape the structure of farm commodity support, expand crop insurance coverage, consolidate conservation programs, revise the Supplemental Nutrition Assistance Program (formerly food stamps), and extend authority to appropriate funds for many U.S. Department of Agriculture (USDA) discretionary programs through FY2017. Senate floor action on the measure is expected in June, as is House Agriculture Committee consideration of its version of a 2012 farm bill.

According to estimates from the Congressional Budget Office (CBO), S. 3240 cuts $23.6 billion over 10 years (FY2013-FY2022) from the March 2012 CBO baseline, largely from the commodity programs—through the proposed elimination of direct, counter-cyclical, and ACRE payments—but also from conservation and nutrition.[1] Crop insurance, horticulture, energy, and research receive increases in mandatory funding.

Below is a brief summary of each of the 12 titles in S. 3240, as filed by the committee on May 24, 2012. This summary is followed by a comprehensive title-by-title, side-by-side comparison of each of the Senate provisions with current law.

Title I, Commodity Programs[2]

The Senate Agriculture Committee-approved 2012 farm bill (S. 3240) restructures farm support for traditional program crops by eliminating direct payments, counter-cyclical price payments, and the "ACRE" revenue program. Some of the 10-year, $50 billion in savings (as estimated by the Congressional Budget Office) within Title I would be used to offset the cost of a new revenue program and to enhance crop insurance in Title XI. Direct payments account for most of current spending and are made to producers and landowners based on historical production of corn, wheat, soybeans, cotton, rice, peanuts, and other "covered" crops.

S. 3240 replaces these programs with a new Agriculture Risk Coverage (ARC) program for covered crops, except cotton, which would have its own program (see "Title XI, Crop Insurance"). In the Senate bill, ARC makes payments to producers for each planted crop when actual farm or countywide crop revenue is below 89% of historical revenue (i.e., the producer absorbs the first 11% of the shortfall). The government then pays for the next 10% of the loss. Any remaining losses are backstopped by crop insurance if purchased by the producer. Authority is continued for marketing assistance loans, which provide price protection at "loan rates" specified in current law (with an adjustment made to the cotton loan rate). The sugar program is left unchanged in the committee bill.

---

[1] For the CBO scoring of the Senate Agriculture Committee bill (S. 3240, as filed by the committee on May 24, 2012), see http://www.cbo.gov/sites/default/files/cbofiles/attachments/s3240.pdf

[2] This section was written by Dennis A. Shields (farm commodity support), Randy Schnepf (dairy), Remy Jurenas (sugar), and Jim Monke (payment limits), all Specialists in Agricultural Policy.

Five disaster programs were established in the 2008 farm bill for weather-induced losses in FY2008-FY2011. S. 3240 reauthorizes four programs covering livestock and tree assistance. Elements of the crop disaster program (Supplemental Revenue Assistance, or SURE) are folded into the new ARC by allowing producers to protect against farm-level revenue losses.

Current farm commodity programs have certain limits that cap payments and set eligibility based on gross income. In S. 3240, the limits are adjusted downward. The bill changes the threshold to be considered actively engaged and to qualify for payments, by limiting the number of farm managers and effectively requiring personal labor in the farming operation.

The Senate bill also contains major changes in dairy policy, including elimination of the dairy product price support program, the Milk Income Loss Contract (MILC) program, and export subsidies. These are replaced by a new program, which makes payments to participating dairy producers when the national margin (average farm price of milk minus average feed costs) falls below $4.00 per hundredweight (cwt.), with coverage at higher margins available for purchase. Participating producers are also subject to a separate program, which reduces incentives to produce milk when margins are low. Federal Milk Marketing Orders continue intact.

Title II, Conservation[3]

The current agricultural conservation portfolio includes over 20 conservation programs. The Conservation title of S. 3240 reduces and consolidates the number of conservation programs while also reducing mandatory funding by $6.4 billion over the 10-year baseline.

Many of the larger existing conservation programs, such as the Conservation Reserve Program (CRP), the Environmental Quality Incentives Program (EQIP), and the Conservation Stewardship Program (CSP), are reauthorized by S. 3240 with smaller, similar conservation programs "rolled" into them. In response to reduced demand and as a budget saving measure, the largest conservation program, CRP, is reauthorized with a reduced acreage enrollment cap using a step-down approach from the current 32 million acres to 25 million by FY2017. CRP is also amended to include the enrollment of 1.5 million grassland acres (similar to the Grasslands Reserve Program, GRP, which is repealed). EQIP, a program that assists producers with conservation measures on land in production, is reauthorized by S. 3240 with a reduced funding level and a 5% funding carve-out for wildlife habitat practices (similar to the Wildlife Habitat Incentives Program, WHIP, which is repealed). CSP, another working land program, is reauthorized at a reduced enrollment level.

S. 3240 creates two new conservation programs—the Agricultural Conservation Easement Program (ACEP) and the Regional Conservation Partnership Program (RCPP)—out of several of the remaining programs. Conservation easement programs, including the Wetlands Reserve Program (WRP), Farmland Protection Program (FPP), and GRP, are repealed and consolidated to create ACEP. ACEP retains most of the program provisions in the current easement programs by establishing two types of easements: wetlands easements (similar to WRP) that protect and restore wetlands, and agricultural land easements (similar to FPP and GRP) that prevent non-agricultural uses on productive farm or grassland. The Agricultural Water Enhancement Program (AWEP), Chesapeake Bay Watershed program, Cooperative Conservation Partnership Initiative

---

[3] This section was written by Megan Stubbs, Specialist in Agricultural Conservation and Natural Resources Policy.

(CCPI), and Great Lakes basin program are repealed by S. 3240 and consolidated into the new RCPP. RCPP uses partnership agreements to leverage federal funding and further conservation on a regional or watershed scale.

Title III, Trade[4]

S. 3240 amends and reauthorizes through FY2017 statutes dealing with U.S. international food aid and agricultural export promotion programs. The Senate bill reauthorizes all of the international food aid programs, including the largest, emergency and nonemergency food aid provided under the Food for Peace Act. The bill contains amendments to current food aid law that place greater emphasis on improving the quality of food aid products (i.e., enhancing their nutritional quality). A new requirement in S. 3240 for food aid to be monetized (i.e., sold in recipient country markets to finance projects) requires implementing partners such as U.S. private voluntary organizations or cooperatives to recover 70% of the U.S. procurement and shipping costs. The bill repeals the specified levels of funds for nonemergency food aid required in current law, but provides increased cash resources to the nongovernmental and international organizations that implement food aid programs.

S. 3240 reauthorizes funding for the Commodity Credit Corporation (CCC) Export Credit Guarantee program and various agricultural export market promotion programs. The bill reduces the value of U.S. agricultural exports that can benefit from export credit guarantees from $5.5 billion to $4.5 billion annually. Funding of $200 million annually is reauthorized for the Market Access Program, which finances promotional activities for U.S. agricultural products, which had been targeted in a number of deficit reduction proposals for elimination. The Farmer Market Development Program (FMDP) continues in S. 3240 at $34.5 billion annually through FY2017.

Title IV, Nutrition[5]

Title IV of S. 3240 largely maintains the nutrition program policies and discretionary and mandatory funding that are contained in the Food and Nutrition Act of 2008 and other nutrition program authorizing statutes.

Provisions in the Senate bill for the Supplemental Nutrition Assistance Program (SNAP, formerly food stamps) include changes to the requirements for retailers who apply for authorization to accept SNAP and changes to some of the rules that govern participants' and retailers' redemption of SNAP benefits. The bill also provides additional mandatory funding for reducing SNAP trafficking, the sale of SNAP benefits for cash or ineligible goods. In terms of eligibility for SNAP and the calculation of monthly benefit amounts, S. 3240 changes how a household's receipt of Low-Income Home Energy Assistance Program (LIHEAP) benefits affects the household's SNAP benefit calculation. It also creates additional disqualification policies for college students and gambling and lottery winners.

S. 3240 doubles funding for Community Food Projects grants and increases mandatory funding for the Emergency Food Assistance Program (TEFAP) by $150 million over 10 years. It also limits eligibility for the Commodity Supplemental Food Program (CSFP) to low-income elderly

---

[4] This section was written by Charles E. Hanrahan, Senior Specialist in Agricultural Policy.

[5] This section was written by Randy Alison Aussenberg, Analyst in Nutrition Assistance Policy.

participants, phasing out eligibility for low-income pregnant and post-partum women, infants, and children. Discretionary authority is added for a Healthy Food Financing Initiative, a financing mechanism to sustain and create food retail opportunities in communities that lack access to healthy food. The bill also provides $100 million in mandatory funding for Hunger-Free Communities Incentive Grants, which funds programs that provide incentives for SNAP participants' purchase of fruits and vegetables.

Title V, Credit[6]

Titles V of S. 3240 restructures the Consolidated Farm and Rural Development Act (also known as the ConAct, the statute that permanently authorizes USDA agricultural credit and rural development programs). USDA serves as a lender of last resort by providing direct and guaranteed loans to farmers and ranchers who are denied direct credit by commercial lenders but have the wherewithal to repay the loan under certain terms. The Senate bill updates and modernizes the statutory language and more clearly organizes the various programs into separate subtitles (new Subtitle A is farm loans; Subtitle B is rural development [see below]; Subtitle C is general provisions). Generally, most provisions are substantially the same, but are renumbered and reorganized.

Changes in the Credit title of S. 3240 include giving USDA discretion to recognize (1) alternative legal entities to qualify for farm loans, and (2) alternatives to meet a three-year farming experience requirement. It increases the maximum size of down-payment loans. It also extends the number of years that farmers can remain eligible for direct farm operating loans, and eliminates term limits on guaranteed operating loans.

Title VI, Rural Development[7]

Like Title V, discussed above, Title VI of S. 3240 is a restructuring of the ConAct, which provides permanent authority for USDA to carry out its portfolio of rural development programs. The Senate bill consolidates various rural water and wastewater assistance programs and the Community Facilities loan and grant program into a new Rural Community Program category, and establishes criteria for which rural communities will receive priority in making loan and grant awards. It eliminates the existing statutory definition of "rural" and "rural areas" for these programs. It also eliminates several business programs, but consolidates many of their objectives into a broad program of Business and Cooperative Development grants.

S. 3240 retains the definition of "rural" and "rural area" for purposes of program eligibility and makes it the basis for all rural development programs. As a result, some areas that previously had been eligible for water and wastewater assistance and Community Facilities loans and grants may no longer be eligible, because the specific statutory definitions of "rural" and "rural area" for those programs have been eliminated. The definition of "rural area" for electric and telephone programs also has been eliminated, and becomes the same as for other rural programs. The bill also retains the 2008 farm bill provision permitting communities that might otherwise be ineligible for USDA Rural Development funding to petition USDA to designate their communities as "rural in character," thereby making them eligible for program support.

---

[6] This section was written by Jim Monke, Specialist in Agricultural Policy.

[7] This section was written by Tadlock Cowan, Analyst in Natural Resources and Rural Development.

Also included in Title VI is the reauthorization of funding for programs under the Rural Electrification Act of 1936, including the Access to Broadband Telecommunications Services in Rural Areas Program and the Distance Learning and Telemedicine Program. The reauthorization also establishes a new grant program for the Access to Broadband Telecommunications Services in Rural Areas Program in addition to its current loan guarantee program. The Delta Regional Authority and the Northern Great Plains Regional Authority are also reauthorized, and various technical changes are made to the organizational structure and operation of the two authorities.

Title VII, Research, Extension, and Related Matters[8]

USDA is authorized under various laws to conduct agricultural research at the federal level, and provides support for cooperative research, extension, and post-secondary agricultural education programs in the states. S. 3240 reauthorizes funding for these activities for FY2013-FY2017, subject to annual appropriations.

New in the bill is mandatory funding of $100 million to establish the Foundation for Food and Agriculture Research, a nonprofit corporation designed to supplement USDA's basic and applied research activities. It will solicit and accept private donations to award grants for collaborative public/private partnerships with scientists at USDA and in academia, nonprofits, and the private sector.

Mandatory funding is continued for the Specialty Crop Research Initiative ($416 million over 10 years) and the Organic Agricultural Research and Extension Initiative ($80 million over 10 years). S. 3240 also provides one-time mandatory funding of $50 million for the Beginning Farmer and Rancher Development Program.

Title VIII, Forestry[9]

General forestry legislation is within the jurisdiction of the Agriculture Committees, and past farm bills have included provisions addressing forestry assistance, especially on private lands. S. 3240 generally repeals, reauthorizes, and modifies existing programs and provisions under two main authorities: the Cooperative Forestry Assistance Act (CFAA), as amended, and the Healthy Forests Restoration Act of 2003 (HFRA), as amended.

Most federal forestry programs are permanently authorized, and thus do not require reauthorization in the farm bill. The Senate bill, however, amends several forestry assistance programs by limiting permanent authority to receive annual appropriations of such sums as necessary and instead authorizing a set level of appropriations through FY2017. It also repeals programs that have expired or have never received appropriations. Other provisions include reauthorizing stewardship contracting, requiring revised strategic plans for forest inventory and analysis, and adding designated treatment areas for addressing insect infestations and disease.

---

[8] This section was written by Dennis A. Shields, Specialist in Agricultural Policy.

[9] This section was written by Megan Stubbs, Analyst in Agricultural Conservation and Natural Resources Policy.

Title IX, Energy[10]

An Energy title first appeared in the 2002 farm bill, and was both extended and expanded by the 2008 farm bill. USDA renewable energy programs have been used to incentivize research, development, and adoption of renewable energy projects, including solar, wind, and anaerobic digesters. The primary focus of USDA renewable energy programs has been to promote U.S. biofuels production and use. Cornstarch-based ethanol dominates the U.S. biofuels industry. However, the 2008 farm bill attempted to refocus U.S. biofuels policy initiatives in favor of non-corn feedstocks; the most critical program to this end is the Biomass Crop Assistance Program (BCAP), which assists farmers in developing nontraditional crops for use as feedstocks for the eventual production of cellulosic ethanol. All of the major Title IX energy programs expire at the end of FY2012 and lack baseline funding going forward.

S. 3240 extends most of the renewable energy provisions of Title IX, with the exception of the Repowering Assistance Program, the Forest Biomass for Energy Program, and the Renewable Fertilizer Study, which are repealed. The bill contains $800 million in new mandatory funding for the FY2013-FY2017 period, including $241 million for the Renewable Energy for America Program (REAP), $216 million for the Biorefinery Assistance Program, $193 million for Biomass Crop Assistance Program (BCAP), and $130 million for the Biomass Research and Development Initiative (BRDI). In addition, $1.125 billion in appropriations is authorized for the various Title IX programs over the five years.

Title X, Horticulture[11]

Title X of S. 3240 reauthorizes many of the existing farm bill provisions supporting farming operations in the specialty crop and certified organic sectors, and expands some of these programs to also support farming operations engaged in local food systems. CBO estimates a total increase in mandatory spending of $212 million (FY2013-FY2017) for Title X. Many of the Title X provisions fall into the categories of marketing and promotion (such as the Specialty Crop Block Grant Program); organic certification; data and information collection; pest and disease control; food safety and quality standards; and local foods (such as changes to the Farmers' Market Promotion Program).

Provisions benefitting these sectors are not limited to Title X, but are contained within several other titles of S. 3240. These provisions would result in further increases in mandatory spending and also authorized appropriations benefitting specialty crop and organic agriculture producers—particularly for programs in the Research and Nutrition titles. Individual programs include the Specialty Crop Research Initiative; the Organic Agriculture Research and Extension Initiative; Integrated Research, Education, and Extension Competitive grants; Section 32 purchases for fruits and vegetables; and new incentives grants. Programs in other farm bill titles include the Value-Added Producer Grant Program, Technical Assistance for Specialty Crops, and the Market Access Program; cost-share and other assistance for organic producers; and provisions in many conservation programs. Other programs are captured within the Crop Insurance, Credit, and Miscellaneous titles.

---

[10] This section was written by Randy Schnepf, Specialist in Agricultural Policy.

[11] This section was written by Renée Johnson, Specialist in Agricultural Policy.

Also in various other titles, S. 3240 authorizes new provisions supporting local food systems, including for beginning farmers. These include assistance and outreach for beginning and socially disadvantaged farmers and ranchers; the Healthy Food Financing Initiative; and mobile technologies. The bill also proposes expansion of the Farmers' Market Promotion Program and reauthorizes funding for the Seniors Farmers' Market Nutrition Program and Business and Industry (B&I) Loans. These changes would result in an overall increase in authorized annual appropriations for programs supporting local food producers and beginning farmers.

Title XI, Crop Insurance[12]

S. 3240 makes several changes to the existing federal crop insurance program, which is permanently authorized by the Federal Crop Insurance Act. The federal crop insurance program makes available subsidized crop insurance to producers who purchase a policy to protect against individual farm losses in yield, crop revenue, or whole farm revenue.

With cotton not covered by the ARC program established in Title I, a new crop insurance policy called Stacked Income Protection Plan (STAX) is made available by S. 3240 for cotton producers. Producers could purchase this policy alone or in addition to their individual crop insurance policy, and the indemnity from STAX would pay all or part of the deductible under the individual policy. STAX sets a revenue guarantee based on expected county revenue. For other crops, a similar type of policy called Supplemental Coverage Option (SCO), based on expected county yields or revenue, is made available by the Senate bill as an additional policy. The farmer subsidy as a share of the policy premium is set at 80% for STAX and 70% for SCO.

Additional crop insurance changes in S. 3240 are designed to expand crop insurance use for other commodities, including specialty crops. The bill requires USDA to conduct more research on whole farm revenue insurance with higher coverage levels than currently available. Another provision makes payments available to producers who purchase private-sector index weather insurance, which insures against specific weather events and not actual loss. A peanut revenue insurance product also is mandated. For conservation purposes, a "sod saver" provision in Title XI reduces crop insurance subsidies and noninsured crop disaster assistance for the first four years of planting on native sod acreage.

Title XII, Miscellaneous[13]

Title XII of S. 3240 includes provisions that cover three areas: socially disadvantaged and limited-resource producers (Subtitle A); livestock (Subtitle B); and other (Subtitle C).

Title XII extends authority through FY2017 for an Office of Small Farms and Beginning Farmers and Ranchers, which was established in the 2008 farm bill to ensure that minorities and limited-resource producers have access to all USDA programs. It also adds military veteran farmers and

---

[12] This section was written by Dennis A. Shields, Specialist in Agricultural Policy.

[13] This section was written by Joel L. Greene (animal agriculture), Analyst in Agricultural Policy; Tadlock Cowan (socially disadvantaged farmers), Analyst in Natural Resources and Rural Development; Jim Monke (USDA data collection), Specialist in Agricultural Policy; and Dennis A. Shields (Noninsured Assistance Program), Specialist in Agricultural Policy.

ranchers as a qualifying group, and reauthorizes funding for the USDA Office of Advocacy and Outreach, which assists socially disadvantaged and limited resource producers.

Within its livestock provisions, Title XII of S. 3240 renews the trichinae certification and aquatic animal health programs that were established in the 2008 farm bill; establishes a grant program for research on brucellosis, bovine tuberculosis, and other priority animal diseases; sets up a grant program to study the eradication of feral swine; and establishes a competitive grant program to improve the sheep industry.

Title XII also makes available higher coverage levels under the Noninsured Crop Assistance Program; establishes a military veterans agricultural liaison office within USDA to provide information to returning veterans on specific programs at USDA; extends a grant program for technological training for farm workers; clarifies conditions for releasing data gathered by USDA to state or local government agencies; provides for an increase in administrative expenses for three regional development commissions that were established by the 2008 farm bill; and includes a provision to remove Canada geese from National Park Service lands near airports to diminish flight safety risks.

Provisions of the Senate Agriculture Committee's 2012 Farm Bill (S. 3240) Compared with Current Law

Title I. Commodity Programs

Current Law/Policy	Senate Agriculture Committee Farm Bill (S. 3240, as filed on May 24, 2012)
Direct Payments	
Direct payments (DPs) are available to producers on farms with base acres (historical plantings) of covered commodities (wheat, corn, grain sorghum, barley, oats, upland cotton, rice, soybeans, and other oilseeds). Direct payment rates are fixed in statute and do not vary based on market price. Covers 2008-2012 crop years. *[7 U.S.C. 8713]* Direct payments for peanuts authorized separately. *[7 U.S.C. 8753]*	Repeals direct payments. *[Sec. 1101]*
Counter-Cyclical Payments	
Counter-cyclical payments (CCPs) are available to producers on farms with base acres (historical plantings) of covered commodities and peanuts. Covers 2008-2012 crop years. Payment rate is difference between target price in statute and national average market price (or loan rate, if higher), minus the direct payment rate. *[7 U.S.C. 8714]* Counter-cyclical payments for peanuts authorized separately. *[7 U.S.C. 8754(a)(1)-(3)]*	Repeals counter-cyclical payments. *[Sec. 1102]*
Revenue-Based Payments	
For covered commodities and peanuts, **Average Crop Revenue Election (ACRE)** payments are available to producers as an alternative to CCPs. Revenue payment based on a two-part trigger: (1) if actual state revenue is less than a guaranteed state level for the commodity, and (2) if actual farm revenue is less than a farm ACRE benchmark for the commodity. Payment amount equals the product of (1) the lesser of (a) the ACRE program guarantee minus actual state revenue or (b) 25% of the ACRE program guarantee, times (2) 83.3% (for crop years 2009-2011) or 85% (2012) of the acreage planted of the covered commodity (not to exceed base acres of the commodity), times (3) the 5-year Olympic average farm yield divided by the 5-year Olympic average state yield (Olympic average drops lowest and highest year). For producers who participate in ACRE, loan rates under the marketing assistance loan program are reduced 30% and direct payments are reduced by 20%. *[7 U.S.C. 8715]*	Repeals Average Crop Revenue Election (ACRE) program. *[Sec. 1103]*

Current Law/Policy	Senate Agriculture Committee Farm Bill (S. 3240, as filed on May 24, 2012)
No comparable provision.	Establishes **Agriculture Risk Coverage (ARC)** program for crop years 2013-17 for the same crops as those under direct payment program (except cotton). Covered commodities are wheat, corn, grain sorghum, barley, oats, long grain rice, medium grain rice, pulse crops (dry peas, lentils, small chickpeas, and large chickpeas), soybeans, other oilseeds, and peanuts. Cotton is not covered under ARC but is eligible for the Stacked Income Protection Plan (STAX) for producers of upland cotton (see Title XI). USDA is required to consider popcorn as a covered commodity.
	USDA makes payments on planted (or prevented from being planted) acres when actual crop revenue (actual yield times national farm price) drops below 89% of the benchmark revenue (see next paragraph). Per-acre payment rate equals the difference between per-acre guarantee (89% times benchmark revenue) and actual revenue. Maximum payment rate is 10% of benchmark revenue per acre.
	For benchmark revenue, farmer can elect either:
	(1) farm level: 5-year farm yield times 5-year average national price (averages exclude highest and lowest years). Payment equals difference between the per-acre guarantee and actual per-acre revenue times 65% of eligible planted acres (and 45% of prevented-planted acreage), or
	(2) county level: 5-year county yield times 5-year average national price (averages exclude highest and lowest years). Payment equals the difference between the per-acre guarantee and actual per-acre revenue times 80% of eligible planted acres (and 45% of prevented-planted acreage).
	The election is a one-time, irrevocable decision applicable to all acres under the operational control of the producers. Eligible program acres cannot exceed average total acres planted (or prevented from being planted) to covered commodities and upland cotton on the farm during 2009-2012. Separate guarantees are to be calculated for irrigated and nonirrigated crops and differentiated by class of sunflower seeds, barley (using malting prices), and wheat. Special minimum prices are established in benchmark revenue calculation for rice ($13 per hundredweight (cwt.)) and peanuts ($530 per ton). *[Sections 1104, 1105, 1107]*

Nonrecourse Marketing Loans and Other Recourse Loans

Current Law/Policy	Senate Agriculture Committee Farm Bill (S. 3240, as filed on May 24, 2012)
Nonrecourse marketing loans are available for any amount of a loan commodity (see list below) produced in crop years 2008-2012. *[7 U.S.C. 8731]* Nonrecourse marketing loans for peanuts are authorized separately. *[7 U.S.C. 8757]*

For peanuts, nonrecourse marketing loans available in crop years 2008-2012. May be obtained through marketing cooperative or association approved by USDA. Storage to be provided on a non-discriminatory basis and under any additional requirements. Payment of peanut storage costs authorized for 2008-2012 crops. *[7 U.S.C. 8757(a)(4)-(7)]* | Generally continues current law to cover 2013-2017 crop years for all loan commodities (including peanuts). *[Sec. 1201]* |

Current Law/Policy	Senate Agriculture Committee Farm Bill (S. 3240, as filed on May 24, 2012)
Loan commodities and loan rates:	Loan commodities same as current law. *[Sec. 1201]*
Wheat, per bushel (bu.), $2.94 ($2.75 in 2008, 2009)	For 2013-2017 crop years, loan rates same as current law except for upland cotton. The loan rate for upland cotton is changed from $0.52 per lb. to the simple average of the adjusted prevailing world price for the two immediately preceding marketing years, but not less than $0.47 per pound or more than $0.52 per pound. *[Sec. 1202]*
Corn, bu., $1.95	
Grain sorghum, bu., $1.95	
Barley, bu., $1.85	
Oats, bu., $1.33	
Upland cotton, lb., $0.52	
Extra long staple (ELS) cotton, lb., $0.7977	
Long grain rice, hundredweight (cwt.), $6.50	
Medium grain rice, cwt., $6.50	
Soybeans, bu., $5.00	
Other oilseeds, cwt., $10.09 ($9.30 in 2008, 2009)	
Dry peas, cwt, $5.40 ($6.22 in 2008)	
Lentils, cwt, $11.28 ($11.72 in 2008)	
Small chickpeas, cwt., $7.43	
Large chickpeas, cwt., $11.28 (not applicable in 2008)	
Graded wool, lb., $1.15 ($1.00 in 2008, 2009)	
Nongraded wool, lb., $0.40	
Mohair, lb., $4.20	
Honey, lb., $0.69 ($0.60 in 2008, 2009)	
[7 U.S.C. 8732 (a)(b)(c)]	
Peanuts, ton, $355 *[7 U.S.C. 8757(b)]*	
Establishes a single loan rate in each county for each kind of "other oilseeds" *[7 U.S.C. 8732(d)]*	
Term of loans: 9 months after the day the loan is made; no extensions. *[7 U.S.C. 8733]* Same term for peanuts. *[7 U.S.C. 8757(c)]*	Same as current law. *[Sec. 1203]*
Loan repayment: Loans may be repaid at the lesser of (1) the loan rate plus interest, (2) a rate based on average market prices during the preceding 30-day period, or (3) a rate determined by USDA that will minimize forfeitures, accumulation of stocks, storage costs, market impediments, and discrepancies in benefits across states and counties. Excludes upland cotton, rice, ELS cotton, confectionery and each other kind of sunflower seed (other than oil sunflower seed). *[7 U.S.C. 8734(a)]* Provides USDA authority to temporarily, and on a short-term basis only, adjust the repayment rates in the event of a severe disruption to marketing, transportation or related infrastructure. *[7 U.S.C. 8734(h)]* Similar provisions for peanuts. *[7 U.S.C. 8757(d)]*	Same as current law. *[Sec. 1204]*
For upland cotton, long grain rice, and medium grain rice, repayment may be at the lesser of the loan rate plus interest, or the prevailing world price for the commodity adjusted to U.S. quality and location. *[7 U.S.C. 8734(b)]*	

Current Law/Policy	Senate Agriculture Committee Farm Bill (S. 3240, as filed on May 24, 2012)
For ELS cotton, repayment must be at the loan rate plus interest. *[7 U.S.C. 8734(c)]*	
For confectionery and other kinds of sunflower seeds (other than oil sunflower seed), loans must be repaid at the lesser of (1) the loan rate plus interest, or (2) the repayment rate for oil sunflower seed. *[7 U.S.C. 8734(f)]*	
Loan deficiency payments (LDP) are available to producers who agree to forego marketing loans. LDP computed by multiplying the payment rate (the amount that the loan rate exceeds the rate at which a marketing loan may be repaid) for the commodity times the quantity of the commodity produced. Loan deficiency payments available for unshorn pelts or hay and silage, even though they are not eligible for marketing loans. ELS cotton is not eligible. Payment rates determined using the rate in effect as of the date that producers request payment (producers do not need to lose beneficial interest). *[7 U.S.C. 8735]* Same provision for peanuts. *[7 U.S.C. 8757(e)]*	For 2013-2017 crop years, same as current law. *[Sec. 1205]*
Payments in lieu of LDP for grazed acreage of wheat, barley, oats, or triticale. *[7 U.S.C. 8736]*	For 2013-2017 crop years, same as current law. *[Sec. 1206]*
Special marketing loan provisions for upland cotton impose a special import quota on upland cotton when price of U.S. cotton, delivered to a definable and significant international market, exceeds the prevailing world market price for 4 weeks. *[7 U.S.C. 8737(a)]* Limited global import quota is imposed on upland cotton when U.S. prices average 130% of the previous 3-year average of U.S. prices *[7 U.S.C. 8737(b)]*	For the period August 1, 2013, through July 31, 2018, same as current law. *[Sec. 1207]*
Economic adjustment assistance to users of upland cotton provides assistance of 4¢/lb. to domestic users of upland cotton for uses of all cotton regardless of origin to acquire, construct, install, modernize, develop, convert, or expand land, plant, buildings, equipment, facilities, or machinery. Effective August 1, 2008, through July 31, 2012 at 4¢/lb. *[7 U.S.C. 8737(c)]*	Same as current law; payment rate drops to 3¢/lb. *[Sec. 1207]*
Special competitiveness program for ELS cotton provides payments to domestic users and exporters whenever the world market price for the lowest priced ELS cotton is below the prevailing U.S. price for a competing growth of ELS cotton for a 4-week period; and the lowest priced competing growth of ELS cotton is less than 134% of the loan rate for ELS cotton. Effective through July 31, 2013. *[7 U.S.C. 8738]*	Same as current law through July 31, 2018. *[Sec. 1208]*
Recourse loans for high moisture feed grains and seed cotton are available for farms that normally harvest corn or sorghum in a high moisture condition at rates set by the USDA. For recourse loans for seed cotton, repayment is at loan rate plus interest. *[7 U.S.C. 8739]*	For 2013-2017 crop years, same as current law. *[Sec. 1209]*

Current Law/Policy	Senate Agriculture Committee Farm Bill (S. 3240, as filed on May 24, 2012)
Adjustments of loan rates are authorized for any commodity (other than cotton) based on differences in grade, type, quality, location, and other factors. Allows county loan rates as low as 95% of the U.S. average, if it does not increase outlays; prohibits adjustments that would increase the national average loan rate. For cotton, loan rates may be adjusted for differences in quality factors. *[7 U.S.C. 8740]; [7 U.S.C. 8758]* for peanuts.	Same as current law. *[Sec. 1210]*
Conservation Compliance/Producer Agreement	
Eligibility for direct payments, counter-cyclical payments, or average crop revenue election payments requires producers to comply with conservation, wetland, and planting flexibility requirements; use base acres for agricultural or conserving use, and not for nonagricultural commercial, industrial, or residential use; control noxious weeds and maintain sound agricultural practices. Producers must submit annual acreage reports for all cropland on the farm. *[7 U.S.C. 8755(a)]* Same provision for peanuts. *[7 U.S.C. 110-246]*, benefits under the marketing loan program are subject to conservation compliance for highly erodible land *[16 U.S.C. 3811(a)(1)(A)]* and for Swampbuster *[16 U.S.C. 3812(a)(1)]*.	Same as current law, with application to the new Agriculture Risk Coverage (ARC) program *[Sec. 1106]* and continued compliance requirement to receive benefits under the marketing assistance loan program. *[Sec. 1201]* For ARC, producer must annually report data on production in addition to acreage. The Secretary shall use data reported by the producer for crop insurance requirements to meet the obligations for program payments without additional submissions to USDA. *[Sec. 1106]*
Supplemental Agricultural Disaster Assistance (Expired on 9/30/11)	
Beginning in 2008, five new disaster programs were authorized for disasters occurring on or before 9/30/11. *[7 U.S.C. 1531]* Program funding derived from a transfer of 3.08% of annual customs receipts to the newly created Agricultural Disaster Relief Trust Fund. *[19 U.S.C. 2497(a)]* The five programs: 1) Supplemental Revenue Assistance (SURE) Payments for crops (not just farm program crops); compensates producers for a portion of losses that are not eligible for an indemnity payment under a crop insurance policy; 2) Livestock Indemnity Program (LIP), which compensated ranchers at a rate of 75% of market value for livestock mortality caused by a disaster; 3) Livestock Forage Disaster Program (LFP) for grazing losses due to drought or fire; 4) Emergency Assistance for Livestock, Honeybees, and Farm-Raised Catfish (ELAP), which provided up to $50 million annually to compensate producers for disaster losses not covered under other disaster programs; and 5) Tree Assistance Program (TAP), which provided payments to eligible orchardists and nursery growers to cover 70% of the cost of replanting trees or nursery stock and 50% of the cost of pruning/removal following a natural disaster. Maximum payments set at $100,000 per person per year for first four programs combined. TAP has a separate limit of $100,000.	SURE is not reauthorized. Other four programs are reauthorized with mandatory funding for FY2012 through FY2017. LIP payment rate is reduced from 75% to 65% of the market value of livestock. Maximum funding for ELAP is $10 million annually. TAP payment rate for replanting is reduced from 70% to 65%. Retains the combined $100,000 per person payment limit for LIP, LFP, and ELAP. Retains the separate limit of $100,000 for TAP. *[Sec. 1501]*

Current Law/Policy	Senate Agriculture Committee Farm Bill (S. 3240, as filed on May 24, 2012)
Payment Limitations	
Establishes the maximum amount of payments per year to a person or legal entity for the sum of all covered commodities, except peanuts. Peanuts have a separate but equal payment limitation. —Direct payments: $40,000 —Direct payments under ACRE: $40,000 minus the reduction required for an ACRE participant —Counter-cyclical payments: $65,000 —ACRE payments: $65,000 plus the reduction in the limit from the direct payment limit. —Marketing loan gains/LDP: no limit. Payments are attributed to a person by accounting for the direct and indirect ownership in any legal entities. Payments made directly to a person are combined with the person's pro rata share of payments from a legal entity. Payments to a legal entity cannot exceed the limits above, and are attributed to persons. Attribution of payments to legal entities is traced to four levels of ownership. If a payment has not been allocated to an individual after four levels of ownership, the payment to the first-level entity is reduced on a pro-rata basis. *[7 U.S.C. 1308, et seq.]* To be eligible for payments, persons must be "actively engaged" in farming. Actively engaged, in general, is defined as making a significant contribution of (i) personal labor or land, and (ii) personal labor or active personal management. Also, profits are to be commensurate with the level of contributions, and contributions must be at risk. Legal entities can be actively engaged if members collectively contribute personal labor or active personal management. Special classes allow landowners to be considered actively engaged if they receive income based on the farm's operating results, without providing labor or management. Spouses are considered actively engaged if the other spouse meets the qualification. *[7 U.S.C. 1308-1]*	Establishes a limit on Agriculture Risk Coverage (ARC) payments, after elimination of direct payments, counter-cyclical payments, and ACRE payments. —ARC payments for the sum of all covered commodities except peanuts: $50,000 —ARC payments for peanuts: $50,000 Continues most other payment limit provisions such as direct attribution, with the exception of the definition of active personal management (see below). *[Sec. 1603]* No provisions for limits on producer subsidies for crop insurance premiums (same as current law). Deletes "active personal management" from the definition of actively engaged in farming. Effectively requires personal labor in the farming operation to be considered actively engaged. Members of legal entities collectively would need to make a significant contribution of personal labor. Adds a special class of "farm managers" that may be considered actively engaged by providing management but not personal labor. However the Secretary would take into account the size and complexity of the operation and whether such management requirements are normally needed by similar operations. A farm manager must the be only person to qualify an operation, may qualify only one operation, and must manage an operation that doesn't share resources with another that collectively receives more than the payment limitations. Separately, clarifies that for the special class of landowner, a "landowner share-rents the land at a rate that is usual and customary" and that government payments are commensurate. *[Sec. 1604]*
Adjusted Gross Income (AGI) Limitation	
Prohibits farm commodity program benefits to an individual or entity if adjusted gross income exceeds certain thresholds. For this purpose, AGI is divided into two parts: farm AGI and non-farm AGI. Uses a 3-year average when comparing to the limit.	Eliminates the distinction between non-farm AGI and farm AGI, and tightens the AGI limit. Prohibits program benefits if the individual's or entity's 3-year average of adjusted gross income exceeds $750,000. Applies to ARC payments, marketing loan gains or loan deficiency payments, supplemental agricultural disaster assistance, and noninsured crop assistance. *[Sec. 1605]*

Current Law/Policy	Senate Agriculture Committee Farm Bill (S. 3240, as filed on May 24, 2012)
—$500,000 limit on non-farm AGI to qualify for and receive any farm commodity program benefits, Milk Income Loss Contract (MILC) program, noninsured crop assistance (NAP), or disaster payments.	No change.
—$750,000 limit on farm AGI to qualify for and receive direct payments. However, counter-cyclical, ACRE and marketing loan benefits may continue if farm AGI exceeds $750,000. *[7 U.S.C. 1308-3a(b)(1)]*	
For FY2012 only, a separate, additional $1 million AGI limit applies to direct payments *[P.L. 112-55, Sec. 745]*	
For conservation programs, $1 million limit on non-farm AGI, unless more than 66.66% of AGI is farm AGI. Provides USDA discretion to waive the limit for "environmentally sensitive land of special significance." *[7 U.S.C. 1308-3a(b)(2)]*	
Sugar Program	
Requires USDA to the maximum extent practicable to operate the sugar nonrecourse loan program at no net cost by avoiding loan forfeitures to the CCC (i.e., no outlays recorded). *[7 U.S.C. 7272 (f), 7 U.S.C. 1359bb (b)(1), 7 U.S.C. 1359cc (b)]* This is to be accomplished by (1) limiting the amount of sugar that processors of sugar beets and sugarcane supply to the U.S. market under marketing allotments, and (2) restricting imports under a quota (see below), in order to maintain market prices above levels supported by loan rates.	Continues all features of the current program and maintains FY2012 loan rates (18.75¢/lb. for raw cane sugar; 24.09¢/lb. for refined beet sugar) through the 2017 crop year. *[Sec. 1301]*
Increases in stages raw cane sugar loan rate from 18.0¢/lb. in FY2009 to 18.75¢/lb. in FY2012, and refined beet sugar loan rate from 22.9¢/lb. in FY2009 to 24.09¢/lb. in FY2012. Continues other provisions found in prior law. *[7 U.S.C 7272 (a, b, c, d, e, g, h, i)]*	Requires USDA, under specified conditions, to operate the feedstock flexibility program for bioenergy producers (i.e., sugar-to-ethanol program) to ensure the sugar program's no-cost directive is met. *[See Sec. 9009 in Title IX -Energy]*
Limits the amount of sugar for food that processors can sell each year (equal to a national "overall allotment quantity" (OAQ) divided between sugarcane and sugar beet sectors, and then allocated to individual processors). Requires USDA each year to set the OAQ at not less than 85% of estimated U.S. human consumption. *[7 U.S.C. 1359aa through 1359jj, 1359ll]*	
For each marketing year, requires USDA by October 1 to set the initial sugar import quota at 1.256 mil. short tons – the minimum spelled out in a U.S. multilateral trade commitment to other World Trade Organization member countries. Stipulates that this quota can only be raised before the mid point of the year (April 1) in case of an emergency sugar shortage caused by a weather disaster, war, or a similar event determined by the Secretary, and specifies the steps that must be followed to increase imports in the event of such a shortage. For each marketing year, grants USDA discretionary authority to increase the sugar quota beginning on April 1. *[7 U.S.C. 1359 kk]*	

Current Law/Policy	Senate Agriculture Committee Farm Bill (S. 3240, as filed on May 24, 2012)
Dairy Programs	
Repeal or Reauthorization of Dairy Programs	
Dairy Product Price Support Program. Mandates the direct support of cheese, nonfat dry milk, and butter at specified prices for five years (through December 31, 2012). Specifies minimum purchase prices of: block cheese, $1.13/lb.; barrel cheese, $1.10/lb.; butter, $1.05/lb.; and nonfat dry milk, $0.80/lb (same levels previously used to support the farm price of milk at $9.90 per hundred lbs. or hundredweight (cwt.)) Allows USDA sale of acquired products when market prices rise to 110% of purchase price. Allows reduction of mandated purchase prices when USDA acquisitions exceed specified levels. Expires on December 31, 2012. *[7 U.S.C. 8771]*	Repealed effective October 1, 2012. *[Sec. 1471(a)]*
Milk Income Loss Contract (MILC) Program. MILC is a counter-cyclical payment program. When the monthly farm price of fluid milk falls below $16.94/cwt., all dairy farmers are paid an amount equal to 45% of the difference between $16.94 and the lower market price. Payments per farm are limited to 2.985 million lbs. of annual production for the period October 1, 2008 through August 31, 2012. For the month of September 2012, the payment factor and the payment quantity are 34% and 2.4 million pounds, respectively. The $16.94/cwt. threshold price must be adjusted upward whenever feed costs are above $7.35/cwt. Beginning on September 1, 2012, the Nat'l. Avg. Dairy Feed Ration Cost trigger rises from $7.35/cwt. to $9.50/cwt. MILC program expires September 30, 2012. *[7 U.S.C. 8773]*	Extended temporarily through June 30, 2013, using the 45% rate rather than reverting to the 34% rate for calculating the payment rate. Effective July 1, 2013, MILC is repealed. *[Sec. 1471(b)]*
Dairy Export Incentive Program. Provides cash bonus payments to U.S. dairy exporters, subject to World Trade Organization obligations to limit export subsidies. Intended to counter foreign (mostly EU) dairy subsidies. Expires September 30, 2012. *[15 U.S.C. 713a-14]*	Repealed effective October 1, 2012. *[Sec. 1472]*
Dairy Forward Pricing Program. Authorizes a dairy forward pricing program. Prices paid by milk handlers under the contracts are deemed to satisfy the minimum price requirements of federal milk marketing orders. Applies only to milk purchased for manufactured products (Classes II, III, and IV), and excludes milk purchased for fluid consumption (Class I). Expires on September 30, 2012. Allows for new contracts until September 30, 2012, but no contract can extend beyond September 30, 2015. *[7 U.S.C. 8772]*	Extended through FY2017. Allows for new contracts until September 30, 2017, but no contract can extend beyond September 30, 2020. *[Sec. 1473]*
Dairy Indemnity Program. Authorizes payments to dairy farmers when a public regulatory agency directs removal of their raw milk from the market because of contamination by pesticides, nuclear radiation or fallout, or toxic substances and other chemical residues. Expires December 31, 2012. *[7 U.S.C. 4501]*	Extended through FY2017. *[Sec. 1474]*

Current Law/Policy	Senate Agriculture Committee Farm Bill (S. 3240, as filed on May 24, 2012)
Dairy Promotion and Research Program. The Dairy Producer Stabilization Act of 1983 authorized a generic dairy product promotion, research, and nutrition education program, funded by a mandatory $0.15/cwt assessment on milk produced/marketed in the 48 contiguous states. Importers in all 50 states, the District of Columbia, and Puerto Rico must also pay an assessment rate of $0.075/cwt on imported products. Authorizes USDA to issue regulations on time and method of importer payments. Expires September 30, 2012. *[7 U.S.C. 4504]*	Extended through FY2017. *[Sec. 1475]*
Federal Milk Marketing Orders. Federal milk marketing order rules issued by USDA place requirements on the first buyers or handlers of milk, including paying at least minimum prices for the milk depending on its end use. Permanent federal authority to regulate the handling of milk was first provided in the Agricultural Adjustment Act of 1933, and subsequently revised by the Agricultural Marketing Agreement Act of 1937, as amended. FMMOs are established under permanent authority and do not need periodic reauthorization. *[7 U.S.C. 601 et seq.]*	Mandates the establishment of an information clearinghouse (including explicit instructions for the requisite types of information to be made available) for the purposes of educating the public about the Federal Milk Marketing Order system and any marketing order referenda. The aforementioned information should be made available through both an internet site and major agriculture and dairy-specific publications. *[Sec. 1462]*
Federal Milk Marketing Order Review Commission. As established by the 2008 farm bill [Sec. 1509], the FMMO Review Commission is mandated to conduct a comprehensive review and evaluation of (1) FMMO system, and (2) non-FMMO systems.	Provides an option for funding from sources other than annual appropriations. *[Sec. 1476]*
Dairy Market Transparency	
Dairy Product Mandatory Reporting. Dairy Market Enhancement Act of 2000 requires manufacturers to report to USDA the price, quantity, and moisture content of dairy products sold. The 2008 farm bill [Sec. 1510] authorizes USDA to establish an electronic reporting system (subject to available funds), after which increased frequency in mandatory reporting of dairy product sales would be required. Provides for quarterly audits of submitted information and comparison with related dairy market statistics. *[7 U.S.C. 1637b]*	Requirements are added that specify a reporting periodicity of no less frequent than once per month. *[Sec. 1461]*
Definitions	
No comparable provision.	**Actual Dairy Production Margin:** difference between the all-milk price and the average feed cost. *[Sec. 1401(1)]*
No comparable provision.	**All-Milk Price:** the national average price received, per cwt. of milk, by dairy operations. *[Sec. 1401(2)]*
No comparable provision.	**Average Feed Cost:** the average price paid for feed used by a dairy operation to produce a cwt. of milk, as determined by the formula—1.0728 x (corn price per bu.) + 0.00735 x (soybean meal price per ton) + 0.0137 x (alfalfa hay price per ton). *[Sec. 1401(4)]*
	Corn and alfalfa hay prices are monthly prices received as reported by USDA in *Agricultural*

Current Law/Policy	Senate Agriculture Committee Farm Bill (S. 3240, as filed on May 24, 2012)
	Prices. The soybean meal price is the monthly price for central Illinois as reported by USDA in *Market News. [Sec. 1402(a)]*
No comparable provision.	**Consecutive 2-Month Period:** the six 2-month periods of Jan.-Feb., Mar.-Apr., May-June, July-Aug., Sep.-Oct., and Nov.-Dec. *[Sec. 1401]*
No comparable provision.	**Calculation of Actual Dairy Production Margin for the Production Margin Protection Program:** the margin is calculated for each 2-month period as the difference between the 2-month average all-milk price and the 2-month average feed cost. *[Sec. 1402b(1)]*
No comparable provision.	**Calculation of Actual Dairy Production Margin for the Dairy Market Stabilization Program:** the margin is calculated for each individual month as the difference between the preceding month's average all-milk price and the preceding month's average feed cost. *[Sec. 1402b(2)]*
Dairy Production Margin Protection Program (DPMPP)	
No comparable provision.	**Dairy Production Margin Protection Program (DPMPP).** Establishes a dairy production margin protection program with two components: basic margin protection and supplemental margin protection. *[Sec. 1411]*
No comparable provision.	**Participation in DPMPP.** All dairy producers are eligible to participate, but must make an election within 15 months after initiation of sign-up period, whereas new dairy producers must make an election during the 1-year period after their first milk is marketed commercially. A dairy operation may elect to remain in MILC during its temporary extension through June 30, 2013, or to participate in DPMPP, but not both. For those dairy producers that elect MILC, they may at any time make a permanent transfer to DPMPP. An annual administration fee is required for participation in DPMPP as follows: $100 if (milk production) < 1million (M) lbs.; $250 if 1M lbs. to 5M lbs.; $350 if > 5M lbs. and < 10M lbs.; $1,000 if > 10M lbs. and < 40M lbs.; and $2,500 if > 40M lbs. This provision also details deposit and use of the fees and conditions for denial of program benefits. *[Sec. 1412]*
No comparable provision.	**Basic Production History.** Under basic margin protection, the highest annual milk marketings of the dairy operation during any one of the 3 preceding calendar years. Special provisions are made for new dairy operations. Once established, the basic production history does not change over succeeding years. *[Sec. 1413(a)]*
No comparable provision.	**Annual Production History.** Under supplemental margin protection, the actual milk marketings of the dairy operation during the preceding calendar year. *[Sec. 1413(b)]* Special provisions are made for new dairy operations, and for transfer or movement of production history. *[Sec. 1413(d-e)]*

Comparison of Senate Agriculture Committee 2012 Farm Bill (S. 3240) with Current Law

Current Law/Policy	Senate Agriculture Committee Farm Bill (S. 3240, as filed on May 24, 2012)
No comparable provision.	**Basic Production Margin Protection (BPMP).** A payment is made to participating dairy operations whenever the 2-month average actual dairy production margin is less than $4.00/cwt. The **BPMP** payment rate equals the amount that the margin is below $4.00/cwt. (up to a value of $4.00) and is paid on the lesser of: (80% of the **Basic Production History**)/6 or the actual quantity of milk marketed during the 2-month period. *[Sec. 1414]*
No comparable provision.	**Supplemental Production Margin Protection (SPMP).** A participating dairy operation may annually purchase SPMP to protect additional margin beyond the basic $4.00/cwt. *[Sec. 1415(a)]*
No comparable provision.	The optional **SPMP Coverage Level** is available in $0.50/cwt increments up to $8.00/cwt. of total margin protection. *[Sec. 1415(b)]*
No comparable provision.	A participating dairy operation also must elect a percentage of **SPMP** coverage equal to not more than 90%, nor less than 25% of the **Annual Production History** of the dairy operation. *[Sec. 1415(c)]*
No comparable provision.	In addition to the annual administration fee for BPMP, an annual premium for SPMP must be paid equal to the product of the coverage percentage, the annual production history, and the SPMP premium rate per cwt of milk. The **SPMP** premium rate schedule varies based on scale of operations and the level of selected coverage. For the first 4 million lbs. of milk marketings the premium per cwt. is $0.01 for $4.50 margin coverage; $0.02 for $5.00; $0.035 for $5.50; $0.045 for $6.00; $0.09 for $6.50; $0.40 for $7.00; $0.60 for $7.50; and $0.95 for $8.00. For milk marketings in excess of 4 million lbs. the premium per cwt. is: $0.02 for $4.50 margin coverage; $0.04 for $5.00; $0.10 for $5.50; $0.15 for $6.00; $0.29 for $6.50; $0.62 for $7.00; $0.83 for $7.50; and $1.06 for $8.00. *[Sec. 1415(d)]*
No comparable provision.	An **SPMP** payment is triggered whenever the average actual dairy production margin for a 2-month period is less than the SPMP Coverage Level selected by the dairy operation. An SPMP payment, if warranted by market conditions, is in addition to the BPMP payment. *[Sec. 1415(f)]*
No comparable provision.	The **SPMP** payment rate per cwt. is equal to the difference between the selected SPMP coverage level and the greater of either $4.00 or the average margin for the 2-month period. The **total** payment equals the SPMP payment rate x the percentage of coverage selected x the lesser of: (SMP production history)/6 or the actual milk marketings during the 2-month period. *[Sec. 1415(g)]*
No comparable provision.	Rules are established for failure of a producer to pay the BPMP administrative fee or SPMP premiums. *[Sec. 1416]*

Current Law/Policy	Senate Agriculture Committee Farm Bill (S. 3240, as filed on May 24, 2012)
Dairy Market Stabilization Program (DMSP)	
No comparable provision.	**Dairy Market Stabilization Program (DMSP).** Establishes a new program applicable for the purpose of balancing the supply of milk with demand (via reduced payments on milk marketings) when operating margins are low or negative. Participation in **DMSP** is mandatory for all dairy producers that participate in the **DPMPP**. The milk marketing volume used for determining dairy payment reductions under the **DMSP** is formula-based comparing shares of actual milk marketings with the producer's **Stabilization Program Base.** At signup in the **DPMPP**, participating dairy producers elect the calculation method of the **Stabilization Program Base** for their dairy operation as either—(A) the average volume of monthly milk marketings during the 3 preceding months, or (B) the volume of monthly milk marketings for the same month in the preceding year. *[Sec. 1431]*
No comparable provision.	**DMSP Implementation Threshold.** When either: (A) the actual dairy production margin is $6.00/cwt. or less for each of the 2 preceding months, or (B) actual dairy production margin is $4.00/cwt. or less for the preceding one month; then reduced payments on milk marketings under the DMSP are in effect beginning the 1st day of the month immediately following the threshold trigger as announced by USDA. *[Sec. 1432]*
No comparable provision.	**Calculation of DMSP Payment Reductions.** During any month in which the milk payment reductions are in effect, each handler shall reduce milk payments to each participating dairy producer from whom the handler receives milk according to the formula:

(A) Reduction Requirement 1: if the actual dairy production margin per cwt. is < $6.00, but > $5.00 for 2 consecutive months, then payment reductions are based on the greater of: (a) 98% of the Stabilization Program Base, or (b) 94% of the actual milk marketings for the month;

(B) Reduction Requirement 2: if the actual dairy production margin per cwt. is < $5.00, but > $4.00 for 2 consecutive months, then payment reductions are based on the greater of: (a) 97% of the Stabilization Program Base, or (b) 93% of the actual milk marketings for the month;

(C) Reduction Requirement 3: if the actual dairy production margin per cwt. is < $4.00 for any one month, then payment reductions are based on the greater of: (a) 96% of the Stabilization Program Base, or (b) 92% of the actual milk marketings for the month.

Once the **DMSP** has been initiated, the largest level of payment reduction required under (A)-(C) shall be continued monthly until the stabilization program is suspended. However, no payment reduction is made if the dairy operation's milk marketings are ≤ the applicable percentage of the Stabilization Program Base. *[Sec. 1434]* |
| No comparable provision. | **Use of Funds from Payment Reductions under DMSP.** The funds obtained from reduced payments to dairy producers for their milk marketings shall be remitted to USDA |

Current Law/Policy	Senate Agriculture Committee Farm Bill (S. 3240, as filed on May 24, 2012)
	where they shall be used to purchase dairy products for donation to food banks and other programs with an end goal of expanding consumption and building demand for dairy products. USDA shall submit a report at the end of each year to the House and Senate Agriculture Committees concerning the funds received, expenditures, and the impact of the DMSP. *[Sec. 1435]*
No comparable provision.	**Suspension of DMSP Payment Reductions.** DMSP is suspended under any of the following market conditions: (1) the actual dairy production margin is > $6.00/cwt. for 2 consecutive months; (2) the actual dairy production margin is ≤ $6.00/cwt. (but > $5.00/cwt.) for 2 consecutive months, but during that same period either (A) the U.S. price for cheddar cheese is ≥ the world price for cheddar cheese, or (B) the U.S. price for nonfat dry milk (NFDM) is ≥ the world price for NFDM; (3) the actual dairy production margin is ≤ $5.00/cwt. (but > $4.00/cwt.) for 2 consecutive months, but during that same period either (A) the U.S. price for cheddar cheese is > 105% of the world price for cheddar cheese, or (B) the U.S. price for NFDM is > 105% of the world price for NFDM; or (4) the actual dairy production margin is ≤ $4.00/cwt. for 2 consecutive months, but during that same period either (A) the U.S. price for cheddar cheese is > 107% of the world price for cheddar cheese, or (B) the U.S. price for NFDM is > 107% of the world price for NFDM. Once DMSP has been suspended, it may not be resumed until at least 2 months have passed (starting on the 1st day of the following month), or the conditions of Sec. 1432 are met again. *[Sec. 1436]*
No comparable provision.	**Enforcement.** Provisions for enforcing DMSP are specified. *[Sec. 1437]*
No comparable provision.	**Audit Requirements.** Provisions for auditing participating dairy operations and for ensuring handler compliance in the DMSP are specified. *[Sec. 1438]*
No comparable provision.	**Study and Report on DMSP.** Mandates that the Office of the Chief Economist, USDA, undertake a study of the impact of the DMSP on both the dairy product value chain and the competitiveness of the U.S. dairy industry in international markets. Study results should be submitted as a report to the House and Senate Agriculture Committees by December 1, 2016. *[Sec. 1439]*

Administrative Provisions for Title I, Commodity Programs

Authorizes use of funds, facilities, and authorities of the Commodity Credit Corporation (CCC) to carry out Title I. Determinations by USDA shall be final. Allows promulgation of regulations, and adjusting expenditures if they will exceed allowable support levels under the Uruguay Round Agreements. *[7 U.S.C. 8781]*	Same as current law. *[Sec. 1601]*

Current Law/Policy	Senate Agriculture Committee Farm Bill (S. 3240, as filed on May 24, 2012)
Suspends the permanent price support authority of the Agricultural Adjustment Act of 1938 and the Agricultural Adjustment Act of 1949 for the 2008-12 crops (covered commodities, peanuts, and sugar), and for milk through December 31, 2012. [7 U.S.C. 8782]	Same as current law, except applies to 2013-2017 crop years, and milk through December 31, 2017. [Sec. 1602]
Provides payments to "geographically disadvantaged farmers" in insular areas, Alaska, and Hawaii for transporting a commodity or input more than 30 miles. Reimbursement based on federal salary differentials defined elsewhere, with maximum of 25% transportation cost. Authorizes $15 million of discretionary appropriations annually for FY2009-12. [7 U.S.C. 8792]	Reauthorizes through FY2017. [Sec. 1606]
Exempts producers from liability for certain deficiencies in collateral to secure any nonrecourse loan. [7 U.S.C. 7284]	Same as current law. [Sec. 1607]
Requires regulations that describe the circumstances allowing payments to a deceased person to settle an estate, and to stop payments for those ineligible. Requires USDA to reconcile tax identification numbers with IRS data twice a year to determine living status. [7 U.S.C. 7284]	Same as current law. [Sec. 1608]
Any person who receives an adverse program decision from USDA's Farm Service Agency, Risk Management Agency, Natural Resources Conservation Service, or the three USDA Rural Development agencies may file an appeal with the National Appeals Division (NAD), an independent office that reports directly to the Secretary of Agriculture. Its mission is to provide fair and timely hearings and appeals to USDA program participants. [7 U.S.C. 6992]	Same as current law. Adds authorization for the Assistant Secretary of Administration to administer law and regulations that relate to competitive and excepted service position in NAD. [Sec. 1609(a)] Defines matters not subject to appeal. [Sec. 1609(b)]
Requires that assignment of payments must be done in accordance with USDA regulations. [7 U.S.C. 8784]	Same as current law. [Sec. 1611]
Requires tracking of program benefits under Commodity and Conservation titles that are made directly or indirectly to individuals and entities. [7 U.S.C. 8785]	Same as current law. [Sec. 1612]
Requires that, if USDA approves a program document containing signatures of applicants, it shall not subsequently determine it to be inadequate or invalid unless the person signing the document knowingly and willfully falsified the evidence of signature authority or a signature. [7 U.S.C. 8790]	Same as current law. [Sec. 1613]
Provides $50 million of mandatory funds from the CCC to implement Title I. [7 U.S.C. 8793]	Provides $100 million of mandatory funds from the CCC to implement Title I. The Secretary is to reduce administrative burdens to program participants, improve information coordination among USDA agencies, and take advantage of new technologies to deliver programs to producers. [Sec. 1614]

Title II. Conservation

Current Law/Policy	Senate Agriculture Committee Farm Bill (S. 3240, as filed on May 24, 2012)
Conservation Reserve Program (CRP)	
Sec. 1231(a-b) of the Food Security Act of 1985 (FSA) (P.L. 99-198, or the 1985 farm bill), as amended, authorizes the CRP through FY2012. CRP provides annual rental payments to producers to replace crops on highly erodible and environmentally sensitive land with long-term resource conserving plantings. *[16 U.S.C. 3831(a-b)]*	Extends authorization through FY2017. Adds grasslands to list of eligible lands, which is consistent with the consolidation of Grassland Reserve Program (GRP) rental agreements under CRP (also see Sec. 2004 below). Amends eligible land definition for land not enrolled in CRP. *[Sec. 2001(a-b)]*
Sec. 1231(c) of the FSA, as amended, determines the planting status of certain land. *[16 U.S.C. 3831(c)]*	Deletes language allowing land enrolled in the Water Bank Program and cropland expiring in CY2000-CY2002 to be enrolled. *[Sec. 2001(c)]*
Sec. 1231(d) of the FSA, as amended, authorizes the maximum acreage enrollment levels; the program is currently authorized through FY2012 to enroll up to 32 million acres. *[16 U.S.C. 3831(d)]*	Reduces enrollment to 30 million acres in FY2013, 27.5 million acres in FY2014, 26.5 million acres in FY2015, 25.5 million acres in FY2016, and 25 million acres in FY2017. Also caps grassland enrollment at 1.5 million acres between FY2013-FY2017. Gives expiring CRP acres priority enrollment for grassland contracts and at least one grassland sign-up must be offered each year. *[Sec. 2001(d)]*
Sec. 1231(e) of the FSA, as amended, defines the duration of contracts. *[16 U.S.C. 3831(e)]*	Amends language for land devoted to hardwood trees, shelterbelts, windbreaks or wildlife corridors to allow for flexible contract lengths beyond the current 10-15 year length. *[Sec. 2001(e)]*
Sec. 1231(f) of the FSA, as amended, lists priority areas as the Chesapeake Bay Region, the Great Lakes Region, and Long Island Sound. *[16 U.S.C. 3831f]*	Deletes watershed-specific language, but retains the use of conservation priority areas as determined by USDA. *[Sec. 2001(f)]*
Sec. 1231B(a-f) of the FSA, as amended, authorizes a pilot program for wetland and buffer acreage in CRP. *[16 U.S.C. 3831b]*	Renames the pilot program "Farmable Wetlands Program," reauthorizes the program until FY2017, and clarifies language related to constructed wetlands receiving water from agricultural drainage. *[Sec. 2002]*
Sec. 1232(a)(8) of the FSA, as amended, establishes approved use of harvesting, grazing, and wind turbine use on CRP acres. *[16 U.S.C. 3832(a)(8)]*	Deletes language related to harvesting, grazing, and wind turbine use on CRP acres. Adds similar language under Sec. 2004 (see below). *[Sec. 2003(a)]*
Sec. 1232(b & d) of the FSA, as amended, requires a conservation plan on all CRP acres and reduces rental payment for certain authorized uses. *[16 U.S.C. 3832(b & d)]*	Amends conservation plan language by removing possible base acre retirement. Deletes rental payment reduction requirement for certain authorized activities. Rental payment reduction language is added under Sec. 2004 (see below). *[Sec. 2003(b & c)]*
Sec. 1233 of the FSA, as amended, specifies the duty of USDA to make cost-share payments and rental payments. *[16 U.S.C. 3833]*	Deletes the current section and adds new section that specifies the duties of USDA as: making cost-share and rental payments; allowing for emergency harvesting, grazing, and other use of forage without a reduction in rental rate; allowing livestock grazing for a beginning farmer or rancher without a reduction in rental rate; certain permitted activities (harvesting, grazing, and wind turbines) in exchange for not less than a 25% reduction in rental rates. All permitted activities must be consistent with an approved conservation plan. Allows grazing, harvesting, and fire suppression on enrolled grasslands. In exchange for a reduced rental rate, a landowner may install land improvement practices up to one year before the CRP acres expire. This land may not reenroll in CRP for five years. *[Sec. 2004]*

Current Law/Policy	Senate Agriculture Committee Farm Bill (S. 3240, as filed on May 24, 2012)
Sec. 1234 of the FSA, as amended, establishes a framework for calculating annual rental payments. *[16 U.S.C. 3834]*	Allows incentive payments for tree and shrub maintenance. Amends rental payment calculation to include grassland contracts for not more then 75% of the grazing value. Dryland cash rental rates may also be used as a factor for determining annual rental rates. Deletes language allowing for in-kind commodities as a form of CRP payment. *[Sec. 2005]*
Sec. 1235(f) of the FSA, as amended, facilitates the transfer of CRP acres from a retiring owner to a beginning/socially-disadvantaged producer to return land to production, and allows new owner to begin land improvements or start organic certification process one year before CRP contract expires. *[16 U.S.C. 3835(f)]*	Simplifies language and provides conforming amendments to the CRP transition option. See *Sec. 2601(a)* for limits. *[Sec. 2006]*
Sec. 1235A of the FSA, as amended, allows land enrolled in CRP before enactment of the 1990 farm bill (P.L. 101-624, November 28, 1990) to convert vegetative cover to hardwood trees or restored wetlands *[16 U.S.C. 3835a]*	Repeals a provision added in the 1990 farm bill that allows land to be converted from vegetative cover to hardwood trees or restored wetlands. *[Sec. 2007]*
No comparable provision.	Provides transition language for existing CRP contracts. Reductions in CRP acres (*Sec. 2003*) take effect upon enactment. All other amendments take effect on October 1, 2012. *[Sec. 2008]*
Sec. 1241(a)(1) of the FSA, as amended, limits payments for thinning activities to $100 million between FY2009-FY2012 and payments for the transition assistance (see Sec. 1235(f) above) to $25 million for FY2009-2012. *[16 U.S.C. 3841(a)(1)]*	Reduces limit for thinning activities (see *Sec. 2005*) to $10 million between FY2013-FY2017 and increases limit for transition assistance (see *Sec. 2006*) to $50 million between FY2013-FY2017. *[Sec. 2601(a)]*
Conservation Stewardship Program (CSP)	
Sec. 1238D of the FSA, as amended, defines program terms for CSP. CSP provides financial and technical assistance to promote the conservation and improvement of soil, water, air, energy, plant and animal life, and other conservation purposes on tribal and private working lands. *[16 U.S.C. 3838d]*	Deletes definition of 'conservation measurement tools' and moves the definition of 'eligible land' from Sec. 1238E(b) of the FSA, as amended to the definition section. *[Sec. 2101(a)]*
Sec. 1238E of the FSA, as amended, establishes the CSP program for FY2009-FY2014. Eligible land includes private agricultural land, tribal agricultural land (that has been planted to crops four of preceding six years), and nonindustrial private forest land. *[16 U.S.C. 3838e]*	Reauthorizes the program through FY2017. Moves definition of 'eligible land' to the definition section (1238D of the FSA, as amended) and removes nonindustrial private forest land limit of not more than 10% of total annual acres. *[Sec. 2101(a)]*
Sec. 1238F of the FSA, as amended, establishes contract requirements for addressing at least one resource concern upon application and meeting or exceeding the threshold for at least one priority resource concern by the end of the contract. Establishes a ranking criteria of applications, contract provisions, contract renewal, and contract terminations. *[16 U.S.C. 3838f]*	Increases the entry requirement to address two resource concerns upon applying and meeting or exceeding the threshold for at least one additional priority resource concern. Adds expiring CRP acres transitioning to production as a consideration for ranking applications. Requires contract renewal participants to agree to, at a minimum, at least two additional priority resource concerns. *[Sec. 2101(a)]*
Sec. 1238G of the FSA, as amended, outlines the duties of USDA, including offering continuous enrollment with at least one ranking period per year, identifying between 3-5 priority resource concerns, and developing a conservation measurement tool. Limits acreage enrollment to 12,769,000 acres for each fiscal year 2008 though 2017. Requires a national average rate of $18 per acre (to include all costs). Payments may be based on the costs incurred, income forgone,	Increases the number of priority resource concerns identified by USDA to not less than five. Removes references to a conservation measurement tool. Reduces the number of enrollable acres to 10,348,000 acres for each fiscal year 2012 through 2021. Adjusts the payment limit requirement to a total of $200,000 for all CSP contracts between FY2013 and FY2017. Provides additional payment direction and requires a prorated performance over the life of the contract to create equal payments each fiscal year. Removes data

Current Law/Policy	Senate Agriculture Committee Farm Bill (S. 3240, as filed on May 24, 2012)
and expected environmental benefits. In general, payments are made at the beginning of each fiscal year and are limited to a total of $200,000 for all CSP contracts during any five year period. [16 U.S.C. 3838g]	collection requirements. [Sec. 2101(a)]
No comparable provision.	Provides transition language for existing CSP contracts. Amendments to CSP take effect on October 1, 2012. [Sec. 2101(b-c)]
Environmental Quality Incentives Program (EQIP)	
Sec. 1240 of the FSA, as amended, authorizes EQIP, stating its purpose as promoting production and environmental quality as compatible goals, and optimizing environmental benefits by assisting producers: (1) with compliance with national regulatory requirements; (2) to avoid the need for regulation; (3) to install and maintain conservation practices; (4) to make cost-effective changes to current production systems, and (5) to reduce administrative burdens by consolidating planning and regulatory compliance . [16 U.S.C. 3839aa]	Removes the 5th purpose area that requires the reduction of administrative burdens on the producer through consolidating conservation planning and streamlining regulatory compliance processes. Adds wildlife habitat improvement and development practices to the 3rd purpose area. [Sec. 2201]
Sec. 1240A of the FSA, as amended, defines six terms: eligible land, National Organic Program, organic system plan, payment, practice, and program. [16 U.S.C. 3839aa-1]	Incorporates the definition of the National Organic Program into the definition of an organic system plan. [Sec. 2202]
Sec. 1240B(a-b) of the FSA, as amended, authorizes EQIP through FY2014. Contracts are 1-10 years in length. [16 U.S.C. 3839aa-2(a-b)]	Reauthorizes EQIP through FY2017. Removes the minimum one-year contract length requirement. [Sec. 2203(1-2)]
Sec. 1240B(d) of the FSA, as amended, limits EQIP payments to not more than 75% of the cost (up to 90% for limited resource, socially disadvantaged farm or rancher, or a beginning farmer or rancher) and not more than 100% of income forgone. Greater significance is provided for determining income forgone payments for specific management practices. Advance payments for certain producers are limited to 30% of the cost share rate. [16 U.S.C. 3839aa-2(d)]	Revises the list of practices afforded greater significance when determining income forgone. Adds veteran farmer or rancher to the list of certain producers eligible for cost share rates up to 90% and advanced payments. Requires advanced payments not used within 90 days to be returned. [Sec. 2203(3)]
Sec. 1240B(g) of the FSA, as amended, requires that 60% of EQIP payments go to practices related to livestock production requirement between FY2008-FY2012. [16 U.S.C. 3839aa-2(g)]	Extends through FY2017 the 60% of payments to livestock production requirement. Adds a minimum of 5% of funds go to payments benefiting wildlife habitat (see Sec. 2203(5)) or $75 million for FY2013, $80 million for FY2014, and $82.5 million for each FY2015-FY2017 (based on levels authorized in Sec. 2601). [Sec. 2203(4)]
Sec. 1240N of the FSA, as amended, authorizes the Wildlife Habitat Incentives Program (WHIP), providing cost-sharing to landowners who improve habitat. Authorized to receive mandatory funding of $85 million annually through FY2012. [16 U.S.C. 3839bb-1]	Adds a new provision under EQIP specifically for wildlife habitat incentive practices. Language is similar to the Wildlife Habitat Incentives Program, which is repealed in Sec. 2707. [Sec. 2203(5)] Funding for the provision is provided in Sec. 2203(4).
Sec. 1240C(b) of the FSA, as amended, identifies priorities to program applications. Gives higher priority for producers using cost-effective conservation practices to achieve environmental benefits. [16 U.S.C. 3839aa-3(b)]	Changes "environmental benefits" to "conservation benefits." [Sec. 2204]
Sec. 1240D(2) of the FSA, as amended, states that in exchange for EQIP	Changes "farm, ranch, or forest" land to "enrolled" land. [Sec. 2205]

Current Law/Policy	Senate Agriculture Committee Farm Bill (S. 3240, as filed on May 24, 2012)
payments, producers will not conduct any practices on the farm, ranch, or forest land that could defeat the purpose of the program. *[16 U.S.C. 3839aa-4(2)]*	
Sec. 1240G of the FSA, as amended, limits EQIP participant's payments to $300,000 for any six-year period. This may be raised to up to $450,000 for any six-year period if the contract is of environmental significance. *[16 U.S.C. 3839aa-7]*	Limits EQIP payments for the period of authorization (FY2013-FY2017) rather than a rolling six-year period. *[Sec. 2206]*
Sec. 1240H of the FSA, as amended, authorizes a competitive grants program within EQIP, known as the Conservation Innovation Grants (CIG). Grants are provided, on a matching basis, to implement innovative conservation practices. Provides $37.5 million of EQIP funds annually (FY2009-2012) to address air quality concerns. *[16 U.S.C. 3839aa-8]*	Deletes the air quality funding carve-out. Adds a reporting requirement that no later than Dec. 31, 2013, and every 2 years thereafter, a report must be submitted to Congress regarding CIG funding, project results, and technology transfer efforts. *[Sec. 2207]*
No comparable provision.	Provides transition language for existing EQIP contracts. Amendments to EQIP take effect on October 1, 2012. *[Sec. 2208]*
Sec. 1241(a)(6) of the FSA, as amended, authorizes mandatory EQIP funding, rising from $1.2 billion in FY2008 to $1.75 billion in FY2014. *[16 U.S.C. 3841(a)(6)]*	Authorizes mandatory EQIP funding: $1.5 billion (FY2013); $1.6 billion (FY2014); and $1.65 billion (each FY2015-FY2017). Amended Sec. 1241(a)(5). *[Sec. 2601(a)]*
Agricultural Conservation Easement Program (ACEP)	
No directly comparable provision. Similar to the establishment and purposes section of the Wetlands Reserve Program (WRP, Sec. 1237(a)), the Farmland Protection Program (FPP, Sec. 1238I(a)&(b)), and the Grassland Reserve Program (GRP, Sec. 1238N(a)) of the FSA, as amended. *[16 U.S.C. 3837(a); 3838i(a)&(b); 3838n(a)]*	Establishes the Agricultural Conservation Easement Program (ACEP). Combines the purposes of WRP, FPP, and GRP. Amended Sec. 1265 *[Sec. 2301(a)]*
No directly comparable provision. Similar to definitions found in Sec. 1237 (WRP) and Sec. 1238H (FPP) of the FSA, as amended. *[16 U.S.C. 3837 & 3838h]*	Defines agricultural land easements, eligible entity, eligible land, program and wetland easement. Divides the easement program into two types—agricultural land easements, which includes components of FPP and GRP and wetlands easements, which includes components of WRP. Amended Sec. 1265A *[Sec. 2301(a)]*
No directly comparable provision. Similar to Sec. 1238I (FPP) of the FSA, as amended. Provides for the purchase of conservation easements by limiting the land's nonagricultural uses. The federal cost may not exceed 50% of the appraised fair market value of the easement and entities must contribute a minimum of 25% of the acquisition purchase price. Prohibits bidding down. Requires USDA to include a contingent right of enforcement in the terms of the easement, and that a conservation plan be required for any easements that include highly erodible cropland. Establishes a certification process for USDA to enter into agreements with eligible entities to use FPP cost-share assistance to purchase easements. To become certified, entities must have the authority and resources to enforce easements, policies in place that are consistent with the purposes of the program, and clear procedures to protect the integrity of the program. Agreements with certified entities are a minimum of five years with a review and recertification	Retains much of the FPP easement requirements for cost-share assistance, agreements with eligible entities, certification of eligible entities, including review and recertification requirements. Allows for grazing as a protected agricultural uses, similar to GRP easements. Requires appraisals based on uniform standards of professional appraisal practice or any other industry-approved standard. Requires eligible entities to provide contributions equivalent to the federal share or at least 50% of the federal share if the entity includes contributions from the private landowner. Allows up to 75% federal cost-share for grasslands of special environmental significance. Establishes an evaluation and ranking criteria for applications. Amended Sec. 1265B *[Sec. 2301(a)]*

Current Law/Policy	Senate Agriculture Committee Farm Bill (S. 3240, as filed on May 24, 2012)
required every three years. Agreements with non-certified entities are 3-5 years in length. *[16 U.S.C. 3838i(c)-(h)]*	
No directly comparable provision. Similar to Sec. 1237-1237F (WRP) of the FSA, as amended. WRP enrolls lands through the use of permanent easements, 30-yea easements, restoration cost-share agreements, or any combination thereof. Eligible lands under WRP include: farmed wetland or converted wetland, together with adjacent land, except wetlands converted before December 23, 1985; cropland or grassland that was used for agricultural production prior to flooding from the natural overflow of a closed basin lake or pothole; and possibly farmed wetlands enrolled in CRP that are likely to return to production upon contract expiration. Ineligible lands include CRP acres containing timber stands or CRP pasture established to trees. USDA is required to determine the value of easements and contracts by providing the lowest amount of compensation based on a comparison of the fair market value of the land, a geographic cap, or an offer made by the landowner. Easements with values less than $500,000 must be paid out over 1-30 years; easements with values greater than $500,000 are to be paid out over 5-30 years. Authorized to conduct a Wetlands Reserve Enhancement Program (WREP) for agreements with states similar to CREP. Priority is given to easements based on the value of protecting and enhancing habitat for migratory birds and other wildlife, while taking into consideration costs and future agricultural and food needs. Eligible land cannot have changed ownership in the previous 7-year period unless the new ownership was by will, succession, foreclosure, or USDA is assured the land was not acquired for the purpose of enrolling in WRP. *[16 U.S.C. 3837-3837f]*	Retains much of the WRP easement requirements for land eligibility, easement terms, compatible uses, easement compensation, violation procedures, duties of USDA and the owner, cost-share, restoration, and technical assistance requirements, and modification and termination procedures. Reauthorizes WREP-like program referred to as the wetland enhancement option. No longer allows for cost-share restoration agreements, only 30-year easements, permanent easements (or maximum duration allowed under law), and 30-year contracts for Indian Tribes. Requires the establishment of an evaluation and ranking criteria that maximizes the benefit of federal investment. Retains priority for easements based on the value to protecting and enhancing habitat for migratory birds and other wildlife, but removes consideration for costs and future agricultural and food needs. Makes the reserved grazing rights pilot program permanent. Compensation provisions are similar to WRP, but adds a requirement that 30-year contract (Tribes only) and 30-year easement compensation be between 50% and 75% of a permanent easement's compensation. Payment schedules are changed for easements with values less than $500,000 to be paid out not more than ten years and easements with values greater than $500,000 to be paid out over 5-10 years. Easement administration may still be delegated, however, the monitoring and enforcement responsibilities may not. Reduces the land ownership requirement to the preceding 24-month period. Amended Sec. 1265C *[Sec. 2301(a)]*
No comparable provision.	Outlines administrative requirements for ACEP using elements of WRP, FPP, and GRP. Provides priority for expiring CRP acres to enter into one) agricultural land easements if it is grasslands that would benefit from long-term easements, or 2) wetland easements if it is a wetland with the highest functions and value that could return to production after leaving the CRP. Allocates funding to no less than 40% for agricultural land easements each fiscal year. Amended Sec. 1265D *[Sec. 2301(a)]*
No comparable provision.	Provides technical amendments for other sections. Amendments take effect on October 1, 2012. *[Sec. 2301(b-c)]*
No directly comparable provision. Sec. 1241(a)(2) and (a)(5) of the FSA, as amended, authorizes mandatory funding to enroll WRP & GRP acres respectively. Sec. 1241(a)(4) authorizes mandatory FPP funding, rising from $97 million in FY2008 to $200 million in FY2014. *[16 U.S.C. 3841(a)(2); (a)(4); (a)(5)]*	Authorizes mandatory ACEP funding: $450 million (FY2013), $475 million (FY2014); $500 million (FY2015); $525 million (FY2016); and $250 million (FY2017). Amended Sec. 1241(a)(2). *[Sec. 2601(a)]*

Current Law/Policy	Senate Agriculture Committee Farm Bill (S. 3240, as filed on May 24, 2012)
Regional Conservation Partnership Program (RCPP)	
No directly comparable provision. Includes elements of the establishment and purposes section of the Agricultural Water Enhancement Program (AWEP, Sec. 1240I)), the Chesapeake Bay Watershed program (Sec. 1240Q), the Cooperative Conservation Partnership Initiative (CCPI, Sec. 1243) and the Great Lakes basin program for soil erosion and sediment control (Sec. 1240P) of the FSA, as amended. *[16 U.S.C. 3839aa–9; 3839bb–4; 3843; 3839bb–3]*	Establishes the Regional Conservation Partnership Program (RCPP). Combines the purposes of AWEP, the Chesapeake Bay Watershed program, CCPI, and the Great Lakes basin program to further conservation, restoration, and sustainability on a regional or watershed scale, and encourage partners to cooperate with producers in meeting or avoiding regulatory requirements and implementing projects. Amended Sec. 1271 *[Sec. 2401]*
No directly comparable provision. Includes elements of previously mentioned programs.	Defines covered programs as ACEP, EQIP & CSP. Eligible activities include those that address water quality and quantity concerns, wildlife habitat, erosion, and others determined by USDA. Eligible partners include state or local governments, Indian tribes, farmer cooperatives, organizations with a history of working with producers on conservation projects. Amended Sec. 1271A *[Sec. 2401]*
No directly comparable provision. Includes elements of previously mentioned programs, primarily AWEP and CCPI.	Authorizes partnership agreements for a period not to exceed five years with a possible one-year extension; describes the duties of partners as defining the scope of projects, conducting outreach, acting on the behalf of producers to apply for assistance, leveraging financial and technical assistance, conducting assessments, and reporting results; partnership agreements are competitive; and provides application content, criteria, and priority. Amended Sec. 1271B *[Sec. 2401]*
No directly comparable provision. Includes elements of previously mentioned programs, primarily AWEP and CCPI.	Directs USDA to enter into contracts to provide technical and financial assistance to producers participating in projects with eligible partners and producers within a project area or critical conservation area independent of working through an eligible partner. Program rules, requirements, and payments are to be consistent with the covered programs (ACEP, EQIP, & CSP). Authorizes up to ten alternative funding arrangements with multi-state water agencies or authorities. Amended Sec. 1265C *[Sec. 2401]*
No directly comparable provision. Sec. 1240(i) of the FSA, as amended, authorizes mandatory AWEP funds of $73 million in FY2009 and FY2010, $74 million in FY2011, and $60 million each fiscal year thereafter. Sec. 1240Q(h) authorizes Chesapeake Bay Watershed program funds of $23 million in FY2009, $43 million in FY2010, $72 million in FY2011, & $50 million in FY2012. Sec. 1243(i) authorizes CCPI to use 6% of covered program for a state (90%) and national (10%) competition. Sec. 1240P(d) authorizes appropriations of $5 million annually for the Great Lakes basin program. *[16 U.S.C. 3839aa–9(i); 3838bb–4(h); 3843(i); 3839bb–3(d)]*	Authorizes mandatory RCPP funding of $100 million annually for FY2013-FY2017, to remain available until expended. Retains the CCPI use of 6% of covered program funds and acres, but amends the CCPI allocation to: 25% for a state competition, 50% for a national competition, and 25% for critical conservation areas (new category). Retains the AWEP and CCPI restriction on paying no administrative expenses of eligible partners. Amended Sec. 1265D *[Sec. 2401]*
No comparable provision.	Requires USDA to make information on selected projects publically available and requires a report to Congress on December 31, 2013 (and every 2 years thereafter) on the status of projects funded. Amended Sec. 1265E *[Sec. 2401]* Requires USDA to use 25% of the 6% made available under covered programs for partnership agreements within no more than eight critical conservation areas (see amended

Current Law/Policy	Senate Agriculture Committee Farm Bill (S. 3240, as filed on May 24, 2012)
No comparable provision.	Sec. 1265D above). Amended Sec. 1265F [Sec. 2401] Amendments take effect on October 1, 2012. [Sec. 2401(b)]
Other Conservation Programs	
Sec. 1240M(e) of the FSA, as amended, authorizes the **Conservation of Private Grazing Land Program**. Authorizes appropriations of $60 million annually through FY2012. [16 U.S.C. 3839bb(e)]	Reduces and extends authorization of appropriations to $30 million annually through FY2017. [Sec. 2501]
Sec. 1240O(b) of the FSA, as amended, authorizes the **Grassroots Source Water Protection Program**. Authorizes appropriations of $20 million annually through FY2012. [16 U.S.C. 3839bb-2(b)]	Reduces and extends authorization of appropriations to $15 million annually through FY2017. [Sec. 2502]
Sec. 1240R of the FSA, as amended authorizes state grants through a **Voluntary Public Access and Habitat Incentive Program** to encourage land-owners to provide public access for wildlife-dependent recreation. Sets application contents and award priorities providing $50 million in mandatory funds for the period FY2009-2012. [16 U.S.C. 3839bb-5]	Reduces and extends authorization for $40 million of mandatory funding for the period of FY2013-FY2017. Requires USDA to submit a report to Congress no later than two years after enactment on the effectiveness of the program. Amendments are effective Oct. 1, 2012. [Sec. 2503]
Sec. 1252 of FSA, as amended, authorizes an **Agriculture Conservation Experienced Service Program (ACES)**, such that USDA can enter into agreements with organizations to provide technical assistance (excludes administrative tasks) using qualified individuals 55 years or older. [16 U.S.C. 3851]	Allows funding for each conservation program in the Food Security Act of 1985, as amended, except CRP, to be used to carry out the ACES program. Amendments are effective Oct. 1, 2012. [Sec. 2504]
Sec. 14(h)(2)(E) of the Watershed Protection and Flood Prevention Act (P.L. 106-472), as amended, authorizes up to $85 million annually in discretionary funding for the **Small Watershed Rehabilitation Program** for FY2008-FY2012 and $100 million in mandatory funding for FY2009 to remain available until expended. [16 U.S.C. 1012(h)(2)(E)]	Extends authorization of appropriations through FY2017. Does not authorize additional mandatory funding. [Sec. 2505]
Sec. 2507 of the Food, Security and Rural Investment Act of 2002 (P.L. 107-171, 2002 farm bill), as amended, authorizes USDA to transfer $175 million of CCC funds to the Bureau of Reclamation to provide water for at-risk desert terminal lakes. [43 U.S.C. 2211]	Deletes current section and replaces with new section that adds definitions for eligible land, program, and terminal lake. Also adds a new voluntary land purchase grant program with authorization to receive $25 million through appropriations to remain available until expended. Retains provisions for voluntary water purchases for desert terminal lakes, including the transfer of $150 million of CCC funds to the Bureau of Reclamation. [Sec. 2506]
Funding and Administration	
Sec. 1241(a) of the FSA, as amended, authorizes mandatory funding through FY2012 (and FY2014 for CSP, EQIP, FPP, and WHIP) to carry out various conservation programs. [16 U.S.C. 3841]	Reauthorizes through FY2017 with funding specified for ACEP and EQIP. Includes payment limits for specific CRP provisions. [Sec. 2601(a)]

Note: Authorized funding levels for various programs are provided in individual

Current Law/Policy	Senate Agriculture Committee Farm Bill (S. 3240, as filed on May 24, 2012)
program sections above.	
No comparable provision.	Allows mandatory funding made available for CRP, ACEP, CSP, & EQIP to remain available until expended. Any funds from a previous fiscal year made available through modifications, cancellations, terminations and other related administrative actions may be reobligated in a different fiscal year, but it will reduce the program's funding by an equal amount in the fiscal year the reobligation occurs. [Sec. 2601(b)]
Sec. 1241(c) of the FSA, as amended, allows CCC funds for conservation programs to also be used for technical assistance. [16 U.S.C. 3841(b)]	Retains a similar provision and requires a report to Congress by December 31, 2012 (and each subsequent year), detailing the amount of technical assistance requested and apportioned for each conservation program. [Sec. 2602]
Sec. 1241(d) of the FSA, as amended, requires that each state receives an aggregated minimum of $15 million annually from certain mandatory conservation programs in order to promote regional equity. [16 U.S.C. 3841(d)]	Eliminates the $15 million annual requirement and allows states in the first quarter of the fiscal year to establish that they can use a total of 0.6% of certain conservation funds. If established, those states may receive 0.6% of funds. [Sec. 2603]
Sec. 1241(g) of the FSA, as amended, establishes an annual set-aside in EQIP and CSP from FY2009-FY2012; 5% to beginning farmers or ranchers and 5% to socially disadvantaged farmers or ranchers. [16 U.S.C. 3841(g)]	Reauthorizes the EQIP and CSP set-aside through FY2017. Provides preference for veteran farmers or ranchers eligible under the provision. [Sec. 2604]
Sec. 1241(h) of the FSA, as amended, establishes reporting requirements for program enrollments and assistance under WRP, FPP, GRP, EQIP, AWEP, CSP, and adjusted gross income waivers. [16 U.S.C. 3841(h)]	Amends reporting requirements to reflect the repeal of WRP, FPP, GRP, and AWEP and the addition of ACEP and RCPP. [Sec. 2605]
Sec. 1244 of the FSA, as amended, outlines administrative requirements for conservation programs including incentives for certain farmers or ranchers, privacy information, conservation plans, acreage limitations, and applications, among others. [16 U.S.C. 3844]	Adds veteran farmers and ranchers to the list of eligible persons authorized to receive incentives. Makes conforming amendments to reflect the new ACEP program. Requires the use of an 'initial application' to reduce duplication, a review and revision of the application process, and notification to Congress when the requirements are complete. Clarifies that conservation payments are in addition to and not included in any payment limit caps. Allows for flexible funding arrangements for Indian Tribes. [Sec. 2606]
Sec. 2904 of the Food, Conservation, and Energy Act of 2008, (P.L. 110-246, 2008 farm bill) requires USDA, in consultation with CCC, to issue rules and regulations implementing Title II provisions within 90 days. Waives certain rulemaking requirements.	Amends and adds the 2008 farm bill regulations provision to a new Sec. 1246 of the FSA. Allows interim final rules to be effective upon issuance. Removes the 90 day promulgation requirement and CCC consultation. [Sec. 2607]
Sec. 1261(b) of the FSA, as amended, requires USDA to develop standard committee operating procedures for State Technical Committees. [16 U.S.C. 3861(b)]	Amends provision to allow USDA to review and update standards as necessary. [Sec. 2608]
Repeal of Superseded Program Authorities and Transitional Provisions	
Sec. 1230 of the FSA, as amended authorizes and establishes the comprehensive conservation enhancement program between FY1996-FY2002. [16 U.S.C. 3830]	Repeals the comprehensive conservation enhancement program. [Sec. 2701]
Sec. 1231A of the FSA, as amended, authorizes and establishes the emergency forestry conservation reserve program within CRP for areas suffering damage	Repeals the emergency forestry conservation reserve program with transition provisions for current contracts to receive CRP funding until expiration. Effective October 1, 2012.

Current Law/Policy	Senate Agriculture Committee Farm Bill (S. 3240, as filed on May 24, 2012)
during the CY2005 hurricanes. *[16 U.S.C. 3831a]*	*[Sec. 2702]*
Sec. 1237-1237F of the FSA, as amended, authorizes and establishes the Wetlands Reserve Program (WRP). *[16 U.S.C. 3837-3837f]*	Repeals WRP with transition provisions for current contracts and easements to receive CCC funding until expiration. ACEP funding may also be used. Effective October 1, 2012. *[Sec. 2703]*
Sec. 1238H-1238J of the FSA, as amended, authorizes and establishes the Farmland Protection Program (FPP) and the Farm Viability Program. *[16 U.S.C. 3838h-3838j]*	Repeals FPP with transition provisions for current agreements and easements to receive CCC funding until expiration. ACEP funding may also be used. Also repeals the Farm Viability Program. Effective October 1, 2012. *[Sec. 2704]*
Sec. 1238N-1238P of the FSA, as amended, authorizes and establishes the Grasslands Reserve Program (GRP). *[16 U.S.C. 3838n-3838p]*	Repeals GRP with transition provisions for current contracts, agreements, and easements to receive CCC funding until expiration. ACEP funding may also be used. Effective October 1, 2012. *[Sec. 2705]*
Sec. 1240I of the FSA, as amended, authorizes and establishes the Agricultural Water Enhancement Program (AWEP) within EQIP. *[16 U.S.C. 3839aa-9]*	Repeals AWEP with transition provisions for current contracts and agreements to receive CCC funding until expiration. EQIP funding may also be used. Effective October 1, 2012. *[Sec. 2706]*
Sec. 1240N of the FSA, as amended, authorizes and establishes the Wildlife Habitat Incentives Program (WHIP). *[16 U.S.C. 3839bb-1]*	Repeals WHIP with transition provisions for current contracts to receive CCC funding until expiration. EQIP funding may also be used. Effective October 1, 2012. *[Sec. 2707]*
Sec. 1240P of the FSA, as amended, authorizes and establishes the Great Lakes Basin Program for Soil Erosion and Sediment Control. *[16 U.S.C. 3839bb-3]*.	Repeals the Great Lakes basin program effective October 1, 2012. *[Sec. 2708]*
Sec. 1240Q of the FSA, as amended, authorizes and establishes the Chesapeake Bay Watershed program. *[16 U.S.C. 3839bb-4]*	Repeals the Chesapeake Bay Watershed program with transition provisions for current contracts, agreements, and easements entered into under the program to receive CCC funding until expiration. RCPP funding may also be used. Effective October 1, 2012. *[Sec. 2709]*
Sec. 1243 of the FSA, as amended, authorizes and establishes the Cooperative Conservation Partnership Initiative (CCPI). *[16 U.S.C. 3843]*	Repeals CCPI with transition provisions for current contracts and agreements to receive CCC funding until expiration. RCPP funding may also be used. Effective October 1, 2012. *[Sec. 2710]*
Sec. 1239-1239D of the FSA, as amended, authorizes and establishes the environmental easement program between CY1991-CY1995. *[16 U.S.C. 3839-3839d]*	Repeals the environmental easement program. *[Sec. 2011]*
No comparable provision.	Provides technical amendments and spelling corrections. *[Sec. 2012]*

Title III. Trade

Current Law/Policy	Senate Agriculture Committee Farm Bill (S. 3240, as filed on May 24, 2012)
Food for Peace Act	
Section 202(e)(1) Support for Eligible Organizations. Provides that of the funds made available for Title II emergency and nonemergency food assistance in each fiscal year, the Administrator of the U.S. Agency for International Development (USAID) shall make available to eligible organizations (private voluntary organizations, cooperatives and intergovernmental organizations) not less than 7.5% nor more than 13% to assist them in establishing new programs, meeting specific administrative, management, personnel and internal transportation and distribution costs for carrying out programs, and improving and implementing methodologies for food aid programs, including monitoring and evaluation. *[7 U.S.C. 1722(e)(1)]*	**Set-Aside for Support for Organizations Through Which Nonemergency Assistance Is Provided.** Amends Section 202(e)(1) to increase the funds made available to eligible organizations for administrative and program activities to not less than 13% nor more than 15% of funds available for Title II emergency and nonemergency assistance. *[Sec. 3001]*
Food Aid Quality. Section 202(h)(1) provides that the Administrator of USAID shall use the funds made available each fiscal year from 2009 and subsequent fiscal years to carry out Title II to assess the types and quality of agricultural commodities and products donated as food aid; adjust products and formulations (including the potential introduction of new fortificants and products) as necessary to cost-effectively meet nutrient needs of target populations; and to test prototypes. Authorizes not more than $4.5 million for FY2009-FY2012 to carry out this section. *[7 U.S.C. 1722 (h)]*	**Food Aid Quality.** Replaces and expands Section 202(h)(1) to require that the Administrator use funds available to carry out Title II to assess types and quality of agricultural commodities donated as food aid; adjust products and formulation, as necessary to meet nutrient needs of target populations; test prototypes; adopt new specifications or improve existing specifications for micronutrient food aid products, based on latest development in food and nutrition science; develop new program guidance for eligible organizations to facilitate improved matching of products to purposes; develop improved guidance on how to address nutritional efficiencies among long-term recipients of food aid; and evaluate the performance and cost-effectiveness of new/modified food products and program approaches to meet nutritional needs of vulnerable groups. Extends authority to fund this section through FY2017. *[Sec. 3002]*
Minimum Levels of Assistance. Requires the provision annually of a minimum of 2.5 million metric tons (mmt) of commodities under Title II, of which 1.875 mmt are designated for nonemergency programs under Title II. Both requirements may be waived, under certain conditions, by the USAID Administrator *[7 U.S.C 1724]*	Extends current minimum levels of assistance through FY2017. *[Section 3003]*
Food Aid Consultative Group. Establishes the Food Aid Consultative Group (FACG) composed of the Administrator of USAID, the Secretary of Agriculture, and representatives of eligible organizations, indigenous nongovernmental organizations in recipient countries, U.S. producer groups, and representatives of the maritime transport sector who review overall program effectiveness. *[7 U.S.C. 1725]*	Reauthorizes FACG through December 31, 2017. *[Sec. 3004]*

Current Law/Policy	Senate Agriculture Committee Farm Bill (S. 3240, as filed on May 24, 2012)
Administration. Sec. 403. Provides for program oversight, monitoring, and evaluation, and requires that systems be established to accomplish these tasks. Requires an implementation report be prepared, to be reviewed by GAO, along with annual reporting. Authorizes appropriations up to $22 million of Title II funds be made available annually (FY2008-12). Requires procedures be developed for providing commodities overseas in a timely manner and according to delivery schedules. Authorizes use of up to $8 million of Title II funds to be used for the Famine Early Warning System Network. Authorizes $2.5 million (of the $22 million) to upgrade information technology systems in FY2009 to enhance monitoring of Title II non-emergency programs. *[7 U.S.C. 1726a]*	**Oversight, Monitoring and Evaluation of Food for Peace Act Programs.** Amends Sec. 403 to authorize activities under this section during the period FY2013 through FY2017. Removes requirements that GAO undertake a study of USAID's oversight of nonemergency food aid programs. *[Sec. 3005]*
Assistance for Stockpiling and Rapid Transportation, Delivery, and Distribution of Shelf-Stable Prepackaged Foods. Authorizes grants for this assistance of $8 million each FY2008-2012. *[7 U.S.C. 1726bf(f)]*	Reauthorizes this provision through FY2017. *[Sec. 3006]*
No comparable provision	**Limitation on Total Volume of Commodities Monetized.** Amends Section 403 General Provisions of the Food for Peace Act [7 U.S.C. 1733] to require that the rate of return for a commodity monetized (sold in recipient countries) be at least 70%. The "rate of return" is defined as equal to the proportion that the proceeds the implementing partners generate through monetization bears to the cost to the Federal Government to procure and ship the commodities to a recipient country for monetization. The USAID Administrator may waive this requirement but report the reasons for granting the waiver and other information to House and Senate Agriculture Committees, House Foreign Affairs, Senate Foreign Relations, and House and Senate Appropriations Committees. *[Sec. 3007]*
Use of Commodity Credit Corporation. Sec. 406 of the Food for Peace Act permits the Commodity Credit Corporation to pay for costs associated with commodities made available, including cost of acquisition, costs of packaging, enrichment, preservation or fortification; costs of processing, transportation, and handling up to the time of delivery to U.S. ports; freight charges from U.S. ports (or designated Canadian transshipment ports) to ports of entry abroad; and costs of ocean transport. *[7 U.S.C. 1736]*	**Flexibility.** Revises Sec. 406 of the Food for Peace Act to permit use of funds available under the Food for Peace Act to pay costs of up to 20% of activities conducted in recipient countries by nonprofit voluntary organizations, cooperative, or intergovernmental organizations. *[Sec. 3008]*
Prepositioning of Commodities in the United States and Foreign Countries. Sec. 407 authorizes the use of available funds to procure, transport and store agricultural commodities for prepositioning in the U.S. and abroad. Authorizes USAID to use Title II funds to procure transport, and store commodities for prepositioning. Authorizes to be appropriated up to $10 million in each of FY2008 through FY2012 for these purposes. *[7 U.S.C. 1736(c)(4)]*	Extends authority for Sec. 407 until 2017. Authorizes from $10 million to $15 million for prepositioning. *[Sec. 3009]*
Expiration Date. Provides that no agreement under the Food for Peace Act shall be entered into after December 31, 2012.	**Deadline for Agreements to Finance Sales or to Provide Other Assistance.** Extends authority to enter into agreements to December 31, 2017. *[Sec. 3010]*

Current Law/Policy	Senate Agriculture Committee Farm Bill (S. 3240, as filed on May 24, 2012)
Authorization of Appropriations. Sec. 412(e) specifies that of the funds available for programs under the act, not less than $375 million (FY2009), $400 million (FY2010), $425 million (FY2011), and $450 million (FY2012) shall be expended for nonemergency food aid. This requirement can be waived only if the President determines that an extraordinary food emergency exists, that resources from the Bill Emerson Trust (see below) have been exhausted, and the President has submitted a request for additional appropriations to Congress equal to the amount needed to reach the required spending level for nonemergency food aid and the amount exhausted under the Emerson Trust. *[7 U.S.C. 1736f]*	**Minimum Level of Nonemergency Food Assistance.** Repeals Section 412(e) and requires that of funds made available under the Food for Peace Act, not less than 15% nor more than 30% shall be expended for nonemergency food aid under Title II. Further, the amount made available to carry out nonemergency food aid programs under Title II shall not be less than $275 million for any fiscal year. *[Sec. 3011]*
Micronutrient Fortification Programs. Section 415 of the Food for Peace Act establishes a micronutrient fortification program for food aid provided to recipient countries through fiscal year 2012 *[7 U.S.C. 1736g-2]*	Extends Micronutrient Fortification Programs through fiscal year 2017. *[Sec. 3013]*
John Ogonowski and Doug Bereuter Farmer-to-Farmer Program. Authorizes voluntary technical assistance to raise farm production/incomes in developing and middle income countries, emerging markets, and in Sub-Saharan Africa and the Caribbean Basin. Program is funded at the greater of not less than $10 million or 0.5% of funds available under the act. *[7 U.S.C. 1737*	Extends program through fiscal year 2017 and provides for annual funding of not less than the greater of $10 million or 0.6 of the amounts made available for each of fiscal yeas 2013 through 2017 to carry out the program. *[Sec. 3014]*

Other Food Aid Programs

Current Law/Policy	Senate Agriculture Committee Farm Bill (S. 3240, as filed on May 24, 2012)
Food for Progress Act of 1985. The Food for Progress Act provides commodities to support countries that have made commitments to expand free enterprise in their agricultural economies. *[7 U.S.C. 1736o]*	Extends program through 2017. Applies the flexibility and limitation on monetization of commodities provisions that apply to Title II nonemergency programs.(See Sec. 3007 and Sec. 3008 above.) *[Sec. 3201]*
Bill Emerson Humanitarian Trust. Establishes a reserve of commodities and cash to meet emergency food needs in developing countries when there are unanticipated needs or when U.S. domestic supplies are short. The Trust can be held as a combination of cash and commodities. The commodities in the Trust may be exchanged for funds available under Title II or the McGovern-Dole Program, or for sale in the market. The funds in the Trust can be invested in low-risk short-term securities or instruments. *[7 U.S.C. 1736f-1 note]*	Extends authority to replenish stocks to maintain the Trust until September 30, 2017. *[Sec. 3202]*
McGovern-Dole International Food for Education and Child Nutrition Program. Makes available U.S. agricultural commodities, financial and technical assistance to carry out food for education and child nutrition programs in foreign countries. Authorizes such sums as may be necessary during FY2008-12. *[7 U.S.C. 1736o-1]*	Authorizes such sums as necessary to carry out the McGovern-Dole program for each of FY 2013 through FY2017. *[Sec. 3204]*

Current Law/Policy	Senate Agriculture Committee Farm Bill (S. 3240, as filed on May 24, 2012)
Local and Regional Food Aid Procurement Pilot Projects. Establishes a pilot program for local and regional purchase of commodities for famine prevention to be conducted by USDA with $60 million in CCC funding (FY2009-2012). *[7 U.S.C. 1726c]*	**Local and Regional Food Aid Procurement Projects** Establishes a local and regional procurement program with appropriations of $40 million authorized for each of fiscal years 2013 through 2017. Preference in carrying out this program may be given to eligible organizations that have, or are working toward, projects under the McGovern-Dole International Food for Education and Child Nutrition Program. *[Sec. 3207]*
No comparable provision	**Donald Payne Horn of Africa Food Resilience Program.** Establishes a pilot program to effectively integrate all U.S.-funded emergency and long-term development activities that aim to improve food security in the Horn of Africa. Authorizes $10 million to carry out the pilot project. Requires the Administrator of USAID to report to appropriate committees of Congress on the outcomes of the project. *[Sec. 3208]*
Trade Provisions	
Export Credit Guarantee Program. Authorizes the Commodity Credit Corporation to guarantee the credit made available to finance commercial export sales of agricultural commodities. The CCC is required to make available the lesser of $5.5 billion annually of guarantees or the sum of guarantees supported by $40 million in budget authority plus the amount of guarantees that the CCC can make available from unobligated prior fiscal year balances. *[7 U.S.C. 5641(b)]*	Amends 7 U.S.C. 5641(b) by striking the section and replacing it with the requirement that the Commodity Credit Corporation make available for each fiscal year 2013 through 2017 credit guarantees in an amount equal to not more than $4.5 billion. *[Sec. 3101]*
Market Access Program. The Market Access Program (MAP) provides for CCC funding of export market development for all U.S. agricultural commodities (generic and branded) by eligible trade organizations. Authorizes CCC funding of $200 million annually, Provided also for products that are organically-produced. *[7 U.S.C. 5623]*	Reauthorizes at current mandatory funding levels of $200 million annually through FY2017. *[Sec. 3102]*
Foreign Market Development Cooperator Program. The Foreign Market Development Cooperator Program (FMDP) authorizes USDA establish and carry out a program to maintain and develop foreign markets for bulk or generic U.S. agricultural commodities and products. *[7 U.S.C. 5721]*	Reauthorizes at current mandatory funding levels of $34.5 million annually through FY2017. *[Sec. 3103]*
Promotion of Agricultural exports to Emerging Markets. The Emerging Markets Program (EMP) promotes U.S. agricultural exports in emerging markets. Authorizes direct credits or export credit guarantees of not less that $1 billion each fiscal year 2008 through 2012 for exports to emerging markets. Requires export credit guarantees be made available to establish or improve facilities and services for U.S. products. In addition, authorizes up to $10 million each fiscal year 2008 through 2012 of CCC funding to be made available to carry out technical assistance activities that promote the export of U.S. agricultural products and address technical barriers to trade in emerging markets, technical assistance can include feasibility studies, market research, industry sector assessments, specialized training, and business workshops. *[7 U.S.C. 5622 note]*	Extends EMP through fiscal year 2017. *[Sec. 3203]*

Current Law/Policy	Senate Agriculture Committee Farm Bill (S. 3240, as filed on May 24, 2012)
Technical Assistance for Specialty Crops. Technical Assistance for Specialty Crops (TASC) authorizes USDA to address barriers prohibiting or threatening exports of U.S. specialty crops. Authorizes mandatory CCC funds reaching $9 million annually (FY2011-FY2012). *[7 U.S.C. 5680]*	Reauthorizes at current mandatory funding levels of $9 million annually through FY2017. *[Sec. 3205]*
Global Crop Diversity Trust. Requires USAID Administrator to contribute to the Global Crop Diversity Trust for germ plasm conservation (up to $60 million over 5 years) provided that the U.S. contribution not exceed one-fourth of the total of funds contributed to the Trust from all sources. *[22 U.S.C. 2220a note]*	Reauthorizes U.S. contribution to the Global Crop Diversity Fund for FY2013-FY2017. *[Sec. 3206]*

Title IV. Nutrition

Current Law/Policy	Senate Agriculture Committee Farm Bill (S. 3240, as filed on May 24, 2012)
Food Distribution Program on Indian Reservations (FDPIR)	
Authorizing statute for FDPIR contains discretionary authority for a "Traditionally and Locally-grown Food Fund." These funds are for USDA purchase of traditional and locally-grown foods to be distributed to FDPIR households. Authority to appropriate $5 million annually to this fund for FY2008-FY2012. *[7 U.S.C. 2013(b)(6)]*	Extends FDPIR's appropriations authority for "Traditionally and Locally-grown Food Fund" through FY2017. *[Sec. 4001]*
Supplemental Nutrition Assistance Program (SNAP)	
Standard Utility Allowances. A SNAP household can use a Low Income Home Energy Assistance Program (LIHEAP) payment (regardless of the amount of that payment) to document that the household has incurred heating and cooling costs. This documentation triggers a standard utility allowance (SUA), a figure that enters into the SNAP benefit calculation equation. Unless the household is already receiving the maximum SNAP benefit, a household's monthly benefit can increase if the SUA calculation results in an excess shelter deduction. *[7 U.S.C. 2014(e)(6)(C)]*	Only LIHEAP payments above $10 would confer this potential advantage. Payments of $10 or less would no longer entitle a household to earn a "standard utility allowance" (SUA) during the benefit calculation process. If a household received below $10 in LIHEAP assistance, households would have to present alternate documentation of utility costs in order to have utilities factored into calculating their excess shelter deduction. *[Sec. 4002]*
Student Eligibility. In most cases, college students (attending higher education courses half-time or more) between ages 18 and 50 are ineligible for SNAP. A student enrolled in an institution of higher education more than half-time is eligible for SNAP benefits only if the individual meets one or more of the following qualifications (1) under 18 years old, or age 50 or older; (2) disabled; (3) employed at least 20 hours per week or participates in a work-study program during the school year; (4) a parent (in some circumstances); (5) receiving Temporary Assistance for Needy Families (TANF) cash assistance benefits; OR (6) enrolled in school because of participation in certain programs. One of the program enrollment exceptions is a "SNAP Employment and Training" program. *[7 U.S.C. 2015(e)]*	Adds the requirement that those students enrolled in post-secondary institutions as a requirement of participation in "SNAP Employment and Training," must be enrolled in certain employment-oriented training to qualify for SNAP; specifically, this includes certain career and technical education, remedial courses, basic adult education, literacy, or English as a second language. *[Sec. 4003]*
No comparable provision. Authorizing statute establishes income and asset thresholds for SNAP eligibility, including that lump-sum, non-recurring payments are to be counted as resources (assets) not income. *[7 U.S.C. 2014]*	**Lottery and Gambling Winnings.** Creates explicit ineligibility for households that receive "substantial lottery or gambling winnings" (as determined by USDA) until the household meets the SNAP resources (assets) and income eligibility limits. State SNAP agencies are to establish agreements with the state gaming agency in order to make determinations of winnings. *[Sec. 4004]*

Current Law/Policy	Senate Agriculture Committee Farm Bill (S. 3240, as filed on May 24, 2012)
Retail Food Store Definition. SNAP benefits can be accepted only by authorized retailers. Among other application requirements, USDA authorization of a retailer is based on the retailer's inventory and sales. SNAP law defines a retail food store, and includes within that definition an establishment that either (1) offers, on a continuous basis, a variety of foods in each of 4 staple food categories [defined in 7 U.S.C. 2012(r)(1)], including perishable foods in at least two of the categories, or (2) has over 50 percent of its sales in staple foods. Authority exists to consider the nature and extent of the food business conducted. No statutory policy on a retailer's sales of non-food items (e.g. alcohol and tobacco). *[7 U.S.C. 2012(p)(1), 2018]*	Amends retail food store definition so that perishable foods must be provided in at least three of the staple food categories. *[Sec. 4005(a)]* No retail food store, which has at or above 45% of its total sales in SNAP-ineligible items (specifically alcoholic beverages, tobacco, and hot foods or hot food products ready for immediate consumption other than those authorized in the restaurant option) can be authorized to accept SNAP benefits. Gives USDA the authority "to consider whether the applicant is located in an area with significantly limited access to food" and makes an exception to the requirement if USDA determines that the participation of the retailer is "required for the effective and efficient operation of the supplemental nutrition assistance program." *[Sec. 4005(d)]*
Electronic Benefit Transfer, Manual Vouchers. An electronic benefit transfer (EBT) point-of-sale machine can be provided by the state agency to the retailer at no cost to the retailer (Many retailers choose to purchase credit card machines that also accept EBT). Although SNAP has transitioned to being fully EBT, and paper coupon ("food stamps") are no longer offered, authority exists to accept manual SNAP vouchers. Some small retailers use these rather than acquiring an EBT machine. No statutory requirements regarding unique terminal identification numbers for EBT machines. *[7 U.S.C. 2016(f), 2018(h)(3)]*	Shifts the costs of EBT machinery to retailer. Bars states from issuing manual SNAP vouchers or allowing retailers to accept manual vouchers unless USDA makes such a determination that circumstances or categories of retailers warrant use of manual vouchers. Requires EBT service providers to provide for and maintain "unique terminal identification number information." *[Sec. 4005(b), (c), (d)(3)]*
Replacement of Cards. Permits state agencies to collect a fee for replacement of an EBT card by reducin[g] the monthly allotment of the participating household. *[7 U.S.C. 2016(h)(8)]*	Adds additional measures regarding "the purposeful loss of cards." USDA may require a state agency to decline a request for a replacement card unless the household provides an explanation for the loss of the card. The USDA requirements must include protections for vulnerable individuals (homeless, disabled, victims of crimes). USDA is to assure certain procedures occur and that procedures are consistent with participants' existing due process protections. *[Sec. 4006]*
No explicit provisions regarding non-wired EBT machinery for redemption or online SNAP transactions are included in the authorizing statute. From FY2012 appropriations, USDA is using $4 million to expand EBT point of sale devices at farmers markets. A number of regulations would need to be rewritten or waived to allow redemption via the Internet. *[7 U.S.C. 2016(h), P.L. 112-55]*	**Technology Modernization.** Requires, depending on results of the demonstration project, that USDA authorize retailers with EBT mobile technologies, if retailers meet certain requirements. Requires demonstration project and report to be completed by July 1, 2015 and for USDA to authorize wireless retailers beginning January 1, 2016, unless USDA reports to congressional committees of jurisdiction that it determines that authorization should not be implemented. Mobile technologies are defined as "electronic means other than wired point of sale devices." A similar statutory provision is included for USDA to authorize retailers to accept benefits online, contingent upon results of a demonstration project and a report to Congress. *[Sec. 4007]*
No comparable provision.	**Community-Supported Agriculture.** Makes SNAP benefits redeemable for shares of Community-Supported Agriculture (CSA). In a CSA, a farmer or community garden grows food for a group of local residents—members, shareholders, or subscribers—who pledge support to a farm at the beginning of each year by agreeing to cover the farm's expected costs and risks. In return, the members receive shares of the farm's production during the growing season. *[Sec. 4008]*

Current Law/Policy	Senate Agriculture Committee Farm Bill (S. 3240, as filed on May 24, 2012)
Restaurant Meals Program. States may choose to operate a restaurant meals program, allowing homeless, disabled, or elderly households to redeem SNAP benefits at restaurants that offer concessional prices. States contract with restaurants, and USDA authorizes them as SNAP retailers. *[7 U.S.C. 2012(k)(3),(4),(9)]*	Creates added responsibilities for state agencies, private establishments, and USDA before restaurants may participate in a restaurant meals program. For restaurants that have contracted with the state to accept SNAP benefits before this provision is enacted, the restaurant may continue to accept SNAP without meeting the additional requirements for no more than 180 days. *[Sec. 4009]*
Quality Control. The quality control system measures the accuracy of the eligibility and benefits calculation in SNAP. The American Recovery and Reinvestment Act of 2009 temporarily changed the definition of the quality control error threshold by raising it from $25 to $50 (meaning that SNAP errors lower than $50 would not "count" as errors in the quality control system). USDA made the $50 threshold permanent in regulation in November 2011. *[7 U.S.C. 2025(c); P.L. 111-5; 7 CFR 275.12(f)(2)]*	Sets $25 as the threshold level for reporting SNAP errors in the quality control system. *[Sec. 4010]*
Appropriations. Authorizes appropriations for SNAP and related programs through FY2012. *[7 U.S.C. 2027(a)]*	Reauthorizes appropriations for SNAP and related programs through FY2017. *[Sec. 4011]*
Nutrition Education and Obesity Prevention Grant Program. Formerly SNAP Nutrition Education or "SNAP-Ed," this program provides formula grant funding for states to provide programs for SNAP (and other domestic food assistance program) participants as well as other low-income households. With these funds, "[s]tate agencies may implement a nutrition education and obesity prevention program for eligible individuals that promotes healthy food choices consistent with the most recent Dietary Guidelines for Americans." *[7 U.S.C. 2036a(b)]*	Adds promoting physical activity as an allowable use of the funding. *[Sec. 4014]*
Trafficking. Authorizes civil penalties and SNAP disqualification penalties for retailers that engage in SNAP trafficking (the sale of SNAP benefits for money or ineligible items). USDA enforces those penalties through a variety of activities and funds from the SNAP account. Approximately $8 million each year was obligated for retailer integrity and trafficking in FY2010, FY2011, and FY2012. *[7 U.S.C. 2021(b)(3)]*	Provides USDA $18.5 million annually through FY2017 in additional mandatory funding to track and prevent SNAP trafficking. *[Sec. 4015]*
Community Food Projects	
Permanently authorizes a grant program for eligible non-profit organizations, in order to improve community access to food. Infrastructure projects are an eligible use of these funds. Grants require 50% in matching funds. Provides $5 million annually in mandatory funding for this purpose. *[7 U.S.C. 2034]*	Eliminates eligibility for infrastructure improvement and development projects. Increases funding for community food projects to a total of $10 million annually. *[Sec. 4012]*

Current Law/Policy	Senate Agriculture Committee Farm Bill (S. 3240, as filed on May 24, 2012)
The Emergency Food Assistance Program (TEFAP)	
For FY2009, mandates $250 million in TEFAP commodity purchases. For FY2010-FY2012, the $250 million in FY2009 is to be adjusted for food-price inflation each year. This funding is available only in the year that it is provided. *[7 U.S.C. 7511a(d)]*	Increases funding by +$100 million over 5 years and a total of +$150 million over 10 years. Entitlement commodity funding increases are concentrated in the first 5 years: +$28 million for FY2013, +$24 million in FY2014, +$20 million in FY2015, +$18 million in FY2016, +$10 million in FY2017 and subsequent years. Makes annual commodity funding available for a 2-year period. *[Sec. 4013]*
Authorizes appropriations ($15 million a year through FY2012) for TEFAP "infrastructure grants." Grants are to be made to emergency feeding organizations (emphasizing those serving mostly rural communities) for projects that improve storage, distribution, and other capacity building. *[7 U.S.C. 7511a(d)]*	Extends discretionary authority through FY2017. *[Sec. 4013]*
USDA is to make bonus commodity purchases using CCC and Section 32 funds based on the needs of the agricultural industry. *[7 U.S.C. 612c]*	Permits USDA to also "consider the needs of the states and the demands placed on emergency feeding organizations. *[Sec. 4207]*
Commodity Supplemental Food Program (CSFP)	
Authority to purchase and distribute CSFP foods distributed in CSFP expires at the end of FY2012. *[7 U.S.C. 612c note(a)-(b), P.L. 93-86]*	Reauthorizes through FY2017. *[Sec. 4101-4102]*
Income-eligible pregnant and post-partum women, infants, children, and the elderly (defined as 60 years or older) are eligible to participate in CSFP. *[7 U.S.C. 612c note(g), P.L. 93-86]* (According to FY2011 USDA-FNS data, 97% of CSFP participants were elderly.)	Only income-eligible elderly would be eligible for CSFP. Enrolled women, infants, and children (who are disqualified by this new provision) would be allowed to participate until their certification period expires. *[Sec. 4102]*
Authority for USDA to enter into reprocessing agreements with private companies in order to process commodity foods for donation and distribution to nutrition programs expires at the end of FY2012. *[7 U.S.C. 1431e(2)(A)]*	Reauthorizes through FY2017 *[Sec. 4103]*
Food Distribution for Child Nutrition Programs	
In addition to the minimum ($200 million-a-year) acquisitions required by the 2002 farm bill, USDA is required to purchase additional fruits, vegetables, and tree nuts for use in domestic nutrition assistance programs using Section 32 funds. The added purchases required are: $190 million (FY2008), $193 million (FY2009), $199 million (FY2010), $203 million (FY2011), and $206 million (FY2012 and each year thereafter). Of this money for additional purchases, at least $50 million annually is required for USDA fresh fruit and vegetable acquisitions for schools. (The Department of Defense Fresh Fruit and Vegetable Program ("DoD Fresh") is one of the ways this is accomplished). *[7 U.S.C. 612c-4]*	Establishes that the $50 million fresh fruit and vegetable acquisition requirement remains in effect through FY2017. *[Sec. 4201]*

Current Law/Policy	Senate Agriculture Committee Farm Bill (S. 3240, as filed on May 24, 2012)
The 2008 farm bill provided $4 million (in FY2009) to purchase whole grains and whole grain products for schools and to evaluate this pilot project. [*42 U.S.C. 1755a; Sec. 14222(d) of Public Law 110–246*]	Renews mandatory funding for the Whole Grain Pilot and evaluation; provides $10 million available over 2 years (FY2013 and FY2014.) [*Sec. 4204*]
Senior Farmers' Market Nutrition Program	
Authorizes and provides $20.6 million annually for the Senior Farmers' Market Nutrition Program through FY2012. [*7 U.S.C. 612c-4(b)*]	Reauthorizes and continues to provide CCC mandatory funding of $20.6 million annually through FY2017. [*Sec. 4202*]
Other Nutrition and Food Security Programs	
2002 farm bill authorized and 2008 farm bill extended discretionary authority for a "Nutrition Information Awareness Pilot Program." [*7 U.S.C. 1755a*]	Repeals this section. [*Sec. 4203*]
Authorized to be appropriated such sums as are necessary through FY2012 for matching grants (1) to food program service providers and nonprofits for collaborative efforts to assess community hunger problems and to achieve "hunger-free communities" and (2) to emergency feeding organizations for infrastructure development. Any available funding is to be divided equally between these 2 grant initiatives, and the federal matching percentage is limited to 80%. [*P.L. 110-246, Sec. 4405*] The 2008 farm bill also authorized pilot projects designed to improve the health status of participants, including a mandatory provision of $20 million for "point of purchase incentive" projects. (USDA has since implemented the *Healthy Incentives Pilot* in Hampden County, Massachusetts) [*7 U.S.C. 2026(k)*]	Amends the hunger-free community grants to delete the authority for infrastructure development and adds authority for a second category of "incentive grants" for projects that incentivize SNAP participants to buy fruits and vegetables. Limits federal cost share to 50 percent. Provides $100 million in mandatory funding over 5 years for the incentive grants. Retains the discretionary authority but limits it to $5 million per year for the previous hunger-free communities grant authorities, now called "collaborative" grants. [*Sec. 4205*]
Currently, the Administration administers a "Healthy Food Financing Initiative" (HFFI) by requesting appropriations for several existing statutory authorities in order to provide grants and tax credits to support development of food retailers in underserved communities. Congress provided no funding for USDA for this initiative, but did provide $22 million for the U.S. Department of the Treasury to administer the New Market Tax Credits for retail food outlets. [*P.L. 112-55*]	Authorizes up to $125 million to be appropriated for a "Healthy Food Financing Initiative" to remain available until expended. USDA is authorized to approve a community development financial institution as "national fund manager" that would administer these funds by supporting food retail projects that would "expand or preserve access to staple foods" (as defined within this section) and accept SNAP benefits. [*Sec. 4206*]

Title V. Credit

Current Law/Policy	Senate Agriculture Committee Farm Bill (S. 3240, as filed on May 24, 2012)
Consolidated Farm and Rural Development Act (a.k.a. ConAct) *[7 U.S.C 1921 et seq.]*	Restructures the ConAct by updating language and more clearly organizing the farm and rural development programs into separate titles. Minor changes to some program parameters as described below, though most provisions are substantially the same and renumbered. *[Sec. 5001]* **Note:** *References below cite the new numbering of the ConAct for provisions notably amended by the Senate bill, followed by the section of S. 3240 making the change.*
Farm Loans	
Definitions. A beginning farmer or rancher is defined, in general, as one with less than 10 years of farming experience, meets participation and other requirements especially if more than one person or entity is involved, and owns a farm that is smaller than 30% of the median acreage size of farms in the county. *[7 U.S.C. 1991(a)(11)]*	Replaces "median" with "average" in the definition of a beginning farmer's ownership limitation: "does not exceed 30% of the average county acreage." This would expand eligibility if the average exceeds the median, such as when small farms outnumber larger farms and a few large farms raise the average. Sec. 3002(26) of the ConAct. *[Section 6001]*
Farm Ownership Loans. Authorizes direct and guaranteed loans for farm real estate purchases to eligible producers who do not qualify for credit from other lenders. *[7 U.S.C. 1922-1925, 1927, 1934-1936]*	Substantially the same, except as noted below. Subtitle A, Chapter 1 of the ConAct *[Sec. 5001]*
Allows farm ownership loans for the following types of entities: cooperatives, corporations, partnerships, joint operations, trusts, and limited liability companies. *[7 U.S.C. 1922(a)]*	Gives USDA discretion to allow alternative legal entities to qualify for farm ownership loans. Section 3101(b)(3) of the ConAct. *[Sec. 5001]*
For direct loans, requires at least three years of farming experience and either be a beginning farmer, not have received prior direct farm ownership loans, or not have received a direct farm ownership loan more than 10 years ago. *[7 U.S.C. 1922(b)(1)]*	Gives USDA discretion to allow alternatives to meet the three-year experience requirement for direct loans. Section 3101(c)(1) of the ConAct. *[Sec. 5001]*
Authorizes appropriations for conservation loans through FY2012 *[7 U.S.C. 1924(h)]*	Reauthorizes appropriations for conservation loans through FY2017. Section 3103(h) of the ConAct. *[Sec. 5001]*
Authorizes a down-payment loan program within the farm ownership loan program for beginning farmers and ranchers and socially disadvantaged farmers and ranchers. Maximum down payment loan size is 45% of $500,000, among other terms. *[7 U.S.C. 1935]*	Authorizes the down payment loan program for beginning farmers (Section 3107(a)(1) of the ConAct *[Sec. 5001]*), and mentions socially disadvantaged farmers under administration (Section 3107(d) of the ConAct *[Sec. 5001]*). Increases maximum down payment loan to 45% of $667,000 (Section 3107(b)(1) of the ConAct. *[Sec. 5001]*).
Farm Operating Loans. Authorizes direct and guaranteed loans for purchasing livestock, poultry, equipment, feed, seed, fertilizer, other supplies, financing land or water development, reorganization, and certain other purposes to eligible producers who do not qualify for operating credit at other lenders. *[7 U.S.C. 1941-1949]*	Substantially the same, except as noted below. Subtitle A, Chapter 2 of the ConAct *[Sec. 5001]*

Current Law/Policy	Senate Agriculture Committee Farm Bill (S. 3240, as filed on May 24, 2012)
Allows operating loans for the following types of entities: cooperatives, corporations, partnerships, joint operations, trusts, and limited liability companies. [7 U.S.C. 1941(a)]	Gives USDA discretion to allow alternative legal entities to qualify for farm operating loans. Section 3201(b)(3) of the ConAct [Sec. 5001]
Limits eligibility for direct farm operating loans to 6 years, with a one-time 2-year extension under certain terms at USDA's discretion. [7 U.S.C. 1941(c)(1)(C)]	Limits eligibility for direct farm operating loans to "7 years," adjusted by 1 year for every 3 consecutive years" that a farmer did not receive a direct operating loan after initially receiving one. Section 3201(c)(1)(C) of the ConAct [Sec. 5001]
Limits eligibility for guaranteed farm operating loans to 15 years [7 U.S.C. 1949(b)]. This limit had been suspended through 2010 [P.L. 110-246, Sec. 5103], but since Jan. 1, 2011, has been in effect.	Omits (eliminates) any term limit on guaranteed farm operating loans.
Allows loans to soil conservation districts that cannot obtain credit elsewhere, up to $500,000, for the purchase of equipment [7 U.S.C. 1944]	Omits any reference to conservation districts.
Emergency Loans. Authorizes direct and guaranteed loans for recovery from natural disasters and quarantines declared by the Secretary or Stafford Act emergencies declared by the President. [7 U.S.C. 1961-1970]	Substantially the same, except as noted below. Subtitle A, Chapter 3 of the ConAct [Sec. 5001]
Allows emergency loans for the following types of entities: cooperatives, corporations, partnerships, joint operations, trusts, and limited liability companies. [7 U.S.C. 1961(a)]	Gives USDA discretion to allow alternative legal entities to qualify for emergency loans. Section 3301(b)(3) of the ConAct [Sec. 5001]
Includes equine farmers and ranchers [7 U.S.C. 1961(a)]	Does not mention equine farmers and ranchers in Sec. 3301 or Sec. 3002 (definitions) of the ConAct.
Requires hazard insurance at the time the loss occurred. Provides an exception for poultry farmers who were unable to obtain insurance. [7 U.S.C. 1961(b)(3)]	Omits any exception for poultry farmers in the hazard insurance requirement. Section 3301(d) of the ConAct [Sec. 5001]
Administrative Provisions. Sets other terms, including loan servicing. [7 U.S.C. 1981-2008l]	Substantially the same, except as noted below. Subtitle A, Chapter 4 and Subtitle C of the ConAct [Sec. 5001]
Specifies the method for selling real property that was acquired by USDA to beginning farmers and socially disadvantaged farmers. [7 U.S.C. 1985(c)]	Continues current law, except does not mention socially disadvantaged farmers. Section 3409(a)(1)(B) and (a)(4)(B)(i) of the ConAct [Sec. 5001]
Specifies that USDA shall offer to sell real property not later than 135 days after acquiring it. [7 U.S.C. 1985(c)(1)(B)(i)]	Shortens to 75 days the time period for USDA to offer to sell real property. Section 3409(a)(1)(B)(i) of the ConAct [Sec. 5001]
Authorizes appropriations of $5 million each year through FY2012 for a Beginning Farmer Individual Development Account pilot program. [7 U.S.C. 1983b]	Reauthorizes appropriations of $5 million each year through FY2017. Section 3430 of the ConAct [Sec. 5001]
Authorizes specific loan levels for direct and guaranteed farm ownership and farm operating loans through FY2012, and reserves or targets funding for certain types of borrowers. [7 U.S.C. 1994]	Reauthorizes the same loan levels through FY2017 and continues the same program targets and reservations. Section 3431 of the ConAct [Sec. 5001]

Current Law/Policy	Senate Agriculture Committee Farm Bill (S. 3240, as filed on May 24, 2012)
Credit Programs in Other Laws	
State Agricultural Loan Mediation Programs. Authorizes a matching grant program for states that provide third party mediation services for agricultural credit disputes. Appropriations authorized at $7.5 million annually through FY2015. *[7 U.S.C. 5106]*	Reauthorizes appropriations of $7.5 million annually through FY2017. *[Sec. 5101]*
Loans to Purchasers of Highly Fractioned Land. Authorizes the USDA farm loan program to lend to Indian tribes or tribal corporations to buy highly fractioned land within the reservation. *[25 U.S.C. 488]*	Allows lending to intermediaries that may create revolving loan funds to relend to purchasers of highly fractioned land. *[Sec. 5102]*
Requires certain levels of appraisal for land to qualify for highly fractioned land loans. *[25 U.S.C. 488]*	Simplifies appraisals for purchasers of highly fractioned land by requiring only one appraisal recognized by USDA or the Department of the Interior. *[Sec. 5103]*

Title VI. Rural Development

Current Law/Policy	Senate Agriculture Committee Farm Bill (S. 3240, as filed on May 24, 2012)
Consolidated Farm and Rural Development Act (ConAct) Authorizing statute for USDA's rural development programs. *[7 U.S.C. 1921 et seq.]*	Reorganizes the Consolidated Farm and Rural Development Act (ConAct). Consolidates rural development programs, makes technical changes to various programs, eliminates programs, establishes criteria for prioritizing loan and grants, eliminates the definition of "rural" and "rural area" for water assistance and community facilities. Makes technical changes to the Delta Regional Authority and the Northern Great Plains Regional Authority. *[Sec. 6001]*
	Note: References below cite the new numbering of the ConAct for provisions notably amended by the Senate bill, followed in bold by the section of S. 3240 making the change.

Defining Rural Eligibility

Sec. 343(a)(13)(A) of the Consolidated Farm and Rural Development Act (ConAct), as amended, defines rural as any area other than a city or town with a population greater than 50,000 and the urbanized area contiguous and adjacent to such a city or town.	Retains Sec. 343 (a) definition of rural as any area other than a city or town with a population greater than 50,000 and the urbanized area contiguous and adjacent to such a city or town.
Defines rural and rural area for water and waste water programs as any town, city, or unincorporated areas under 10,000 population.	Eliminates the rural definition for water and waste water projects so that the definition above applies.
Defines rural and rural area for community facility loan and grant program as any area other than a town or city with a population greater than 20,000.	Eliminates the rural definition for community facility loan and grants so that the definition above applies.
Establishes criteria for determining areas as "rural in character" and makes certain exclusions for rural areas that could be classified as lying within an "urbanized area." *[7 U.S.C. 1991(a(13)(A)]*	Amends criteria for determining areas "rural in character" and establishes priorities in making these determinations. Extends the current exclusion for "urbanized areas" where a single road may cause a rural town to be included within an urbanized area. Section 3002 28(A)(i) of the ConAct. *[Sec. 6001]*

Rural Community Programs

Rural Water Loan and Grant Program. Loans and grants to support improvements to rural water systems. Subject to annual appropriations. *[7 U.S.C. 1926(a)(2]*	Reauthorizes funding to make loans, grants, and loan guarantees for the Rural Water and Waste Disposal Loan and Grant Programs. Establishes priorities for rural water programs, including a priority for rural communities of 5,500 or fewer permanent residents. Section 3501 (a)-(d)(f) of the ConAct. *[Sec. 6001]*
Revolving Funds for Financing Water and Waste Water Projects Program. Provides capital to fund revolving loan funds for supporting rural water projects. Authorizes $35 million annually for 2008-2012, subject to annual appropriations. *[7 U.S.C. 1926(a)(2)(B)]*	Reauthorizes funding for Revolving Funds for Financing Water and Wastewater Projects at $30 million annually for FY2013-FY2017, subject to appropriations. Section 3501(e)(1) of the ConAct. *[Sec. 6001]*

Current Law/Policy	Senate Agriculture Committee Farm Bill (S. 3240, as filed on May 24, 2012)
Emergency and Imminent Community Water Assistance Program. Provides assistance to water systems in rural communities where there is a threat to potable water supplies. Subject to annual appropriations. *[7 U.S.C. 1926a(i)(2)]*	Reauthorizes funding for Emergency and Imminent Community Water Assistance Program at $35 million annually for FY2013-FY2017, subject to appropriations. Section 3501(e)(2) of the ConAct. *[Sec. 6001]*
Water and Waste Facility Loans and Grants to Alleviate Health Risks Provides loan and grant support to rural water systems to improve sanitation and potable water supplies. Authorizes an annual appropriation of $30 million in loan subsidies, $30 million in grants, and $20 million in grants specifically for Tribal groups. *[7 U.S.C. 1926c]*	Reauthorizes funding for Water and Waste Facility Loans and Grants to Alleviate Health Risks at $60 million in loan subsidies, $60 million in grants, and $20 million in grants specifically for Tribal groups annually for FY2013-FY2017, subject to appropriations. Section 3501(e)(3)(B) of the ConAct. *[Sec. 6001]*
Grants for Water Systems for Rural and Native Villages in Alaska. Funding for water projects to improve sanitation and potable water in rural Alaska. Authorizes $30 million annually for FY2008-FY2012, subject to appropriations. *[7 U.S.C. 1926d]*	Reauthorizes funding for the program and specifies eligibility for native villages for Alaska and Hawaii for Water and Waste Facility Loans and Grants to Alleviate Health Risks to include Native Tribes, rural or native villages in Alaska and Hawaii. Section 3501(e)(3)(B) of the ConAct. *[Sec. 6001]*
Solid Waste Management Grants. Provides grant assistance for communities to establish or improve solid waste management facilities. Subject to annual appropriations. *[7 U.S.C. 1932(b)]*	Reauthorizes funding for Solid Waste Management Grants at $10 million annually for FY2013-FY2017, subject to appropriations. Section 3501(e)(4) of the ConAct. *[Sec. 6001]*
Rural Water and Wastewater Technical Assistance and Training Grants. Provides funding for technical and managerial expertise assistance from third-parties (e.g., National Rural Water Association Program) to assist rural communities with various water and waste water issues. Authorizes that between 1% and 3% of total water and waste water appropriation be allocated to these grants annually for FY2008-FY2012 *[7 U.S.C. 1926(a)(14)]*	Reauthorizes funding for Rural Water and Wastewater Technical Assistance and Training Grants at the current allocation rate of between 1% and 3% of the total water and waste water appropriation annually for FY2013-FY2017. Section 3501(e)(5) of the ConAct. *[Sec. 6001]*
Special Evaluation Assistance for Rural Communities and Households (SEARCH) Program. Provides grant assistance to communities under 2,500 to help them prepare an application for a water or waste water loan and grant. Up to 4% of the funds appropriated for water and waste disposal projects and essential community facilities may be used to fund SEARCH grants. *[7 U.S.C. 2009ee]*	Reauthorizes funding for the SEARCH Program at such sums as necessary for FY2013-FY2017, subject to annual appropriations. Section 3501(e)(6) of the ConAct. *[Sec. 6001]*
Community Facilities Loan and Grant Program. Provides loan, grant, and loan guarantees for "essential community facilities." Most funding has supported projects for improved community health and safety (e.g., health clinics, elder care facilities, fire protection, emergency responders). Authorizes such sums as necessary annually, subject to appropriations. *[7 U.S.C. 1926(a)(19)]*	Reauthorizes funding for Community Facilities Programs at $10 million annually for FY2013-FY2017, subject to appropriations. Establishes new priorities for Community Facilities loans and grants, including prioritization for communities with less than 20,000 in population. Also authorizes a new Technical Assistance for Community Facilities Program as part of the current Community Facilities Program. Provides technical assistance and planning assistance to rural communities in developing essential community facilities. Reauthorizes such sums as necessary for FY2013-FY2017, subject to annual appropriations. Section 3502(a)-(d)(e)(g) of the ConAct. *[Sec. 6001]*

Current Law/Policy	Senate Agriculture Committee Farm Bill (S. 3240, as filed on May 24, 2012)
Rural Business and Cooperative Development	
Rural Business Opportunity Grants. Provides grant assistance of up to $1.5 million to identify business opportunities that will use local rural resources, to train and provide technical assistance to existing or prospective rural entrepreneurs, to establish business support centers, and to support local and regional economic development planning. Authorizes $15 million annually for FY2008-FY2012, subject to appropriations. *[7 U.S.C. 1926(a)(11)]*	Eliminates the program, but consolidates the program's objectives within a broad rural business development grants program. Authorizes $65 million annually for the broader program for FY2013-FY2017, subject to appropriations. Section 3601(a) of the ConAct. *[Sec. 6001]*
Rural Business Enterprise Grants. Provides grant support of up to $50,000 to public bodies and nonprofit corporations for measures designed to facilitate small and emerging business enterprises, or the creation and expansion of rural distance learning networks, among other eligible activities. Subject to annual appropriations. *[7 U.S.C. 1932(c)]*	Eliminates the program, but consolidates the program's objectives within a broad rural business development grants program. Authorizes $65 million annually for the broader program (as above) for FY2013-FY2017, subject to appropriations. Section 3601(a) of the ConAct. *[Sec. 6001]*
Value-Added Producer Grants. Provides grant support to agricultural producers to undertake projects that add value to commodities and thereby increase producer income. Also supports planning and business development for value-added projects. Subject to annual appropriations from the Rural Cooperative Development Grants program. *[7 U.S.C. 1621]*	Reauthorizes funding for Value-Added Agricultural Producer Grants at $40 million annually for FY2013-FY2017, subject to appropriations. Establishes priority for projects in which at least 25% of the project recipients are beginning farmers or ranchers or socially disadvantaged farmers or ranchers. Section 3601(b) of the ConAct. *[Sec. 6001]*
Rural Cooperative Development Grants. Facilitate the creation of jobs in rural areas through the development of new rural cooperatives, value-added processing, and rural businesses. Authorizes $50 million annually for FY2008-FY2012, subject to annual appropriations. *[7 U.S.C. 1932(e)(5)]*	Reauthorizes funding for Rural Cooperative Development Grants at $50 million annually for FY2013-FY2017 subject to appropriations. Includes directive to coordinate an interagency working group among federal agencies to support cooperative development. Section 3601(c) of the ConAct. *[Sec. 6001]*
Appropriate Technology Transfer for Rural Areas (ATTRA). Provides grant support at an agricultural institution (e.g., universities) for information activities to agricultural producers. Authorizes $5 million annually for FY2008-FY2012, subject to appropriations. *[7 U.S.C. 1932]*	Reauthorizes funding for ATTRA at $5 million annually for FY2013-FY2017, subject to appropriations. Section 3601(d) of the ConAct. *[Sec. 6001]*
Business and Industry Direct and Guaranteed Loans. Provides loans for a wide variety of projects to support business development in rural areas and to increase and retain jobs in rural areas. Subject to annual appropriations. (Note: Direct loan program has not been funded since 2002.) *[7 U.S.C. 1932(a)(2)(A)]*	Reauthorizes funding of $75 million annually for FY2013-FY2017, subject to appropriations. Raises initial fee to 3% from current authorization of 2%. Reauthorizes a 5% carve-out of guaranteed loan authority for Locally or Regionally Produced Agricultural Food Products. Section 3601(e) of the ConAct. *[Sec. 6001]*
Intermediary Relending Program (IRP). The IRP provides direct loans at 1% interest to intermediaries to finance business facilities and community development projects in rural areas of 25,000 population or less. The Rural Business Service loan to an intermediary is used to establish or fund a revolving loan program to provide financial assistance to ultimate recipients for community development projects, establishment of new businesses or expansion of existing businesses. Subject to annual appropriations. *[7 U.S.C. 1932]*	Reauthorizes funding for IRP at $50 million annually for FY2013-FY2017, subject to appropriations. Section 3601(f)(1) of the ConAct. *[Sec. 6001]*

Current Law/Policy	Senate Agriculture Committee Farm Bill (S. 3240, as filed on May 24, 2012)
Rural Microentrepreneur Assistance Program. Provides grant support to third-party entities who assist rural entrepreneurs in establishing microenterprises in rural areas. Authorizes $4 million in mandatory spending for FY2009-FY2011 and $3 million for FY2012. Also authorizes $40 million annually in discretionary spending for FY2009-FY2012, subject to appropriations. *[7 U.S.C. 1981 et seq.]*	Reauthorizes funding for Rural Microentrepreneur Assistance Program at $40 million annually for FY2013-FY2017, subject to appropriations. Section 3601(f)(2) of the ConAct. *[Sec. 6001]*
Rural Business Investment Program. Modeled on the Small Business Administration's Small Business Investment Companies, the Rural Business Investment Program provides funding to help capitalized Rural Business Investment Companies that, in turn, provide loans to rural businesses. Authorizes $50 million for the period FY2008-FY2012, subject to appropriations. *[7 U.S.C. 2009cc et seq.]*	Reauthorizes funding for Rural Business Investment Program at $25 million annually through FY2017 subject to appropriations. Provides authority for USDA to establish capital requirements, establish fees for applicants applying for a license to operate as a rural business investment company, and ensures the majority of capital of each rural business company is invested in rural concerns. Section 3602of the ConAct. *[Sec. 6001]*
Rural Business Collaborative Investment Program. Provides loan and grant support to rural regions to establish regional competitiveness by fostering collaboration among rural businesses, rural institutions, and entrepreneurs. Establishes multijurisdictional and multisectoral Regional Rural Investment Boards and provides Regional Innovation Grants. Authorizes $135 million for the period FY2008-FY2012, subject to annual appropriations. Program was never implemented. *[7 U.S.C 2009dd]*	Eliminates the program.
General Rural Development Provisions	
General authority for USDA to award grants and to make and guarantee loans to various entities *[7 U.S.C. 1926]*	Reauthorizes and contains general provisions for loan and grant authority. Section 3701 of the ConAct. *[Sec. 6001]*
No comparable provision.	**Strategic Economic and Community Development.** Authorizes USDA to prioritize otherwise eligible applications that support strategic economic and community development and establishes criteria for evaluating applications. Section 3703(a)of the ConAct. *[Sec. 6001]*
Rural Development Insurance Fund. Authorizes a revolving fund for the discharge of the obligations of USDA under contracts guaranteeing or insuring rural development loans. Funds not needed for current operations are deposited in the U.S. Treasury for credit to the fund, or invested in obligations guaranteed by the United States *[7 U.S.C. 1929a]*	Continues permanent authority for the Rural Development Insurance Fund. Section 3704 of the ConAct. *[Sec. 6001]*
Rural Economic Area Partnership (REAP). The program assists communities dealing with geographic and economic isolation, low density population, absence of nearby metropolitan centers, historic dependence on agribusiness, out-migration, and economic upheaval to develop strategies for revitalization Zones. *[7 U.S.C. 1932]*	Establishes process for USDA to designate new Rural Economic Area Partnership zones. Section 3705(a) of the ConAct. *[Sec. 6001]*

Current Law/Policy	Senate Agriculture Committee Farm Bill (S. 3240, as filed on May 24, 2012)
Rural Telecommunications and Electrification: Rural Electrification Act	
Definition of Rural Area. Defines rural and rural area to mean any area other than a city or town or unincorporated place with a population greater than 20,000 residents, and any area within the service area of an electric, telephone, or telephone bank borrower under Section 13(3)the Rural Electrification Act. *[7 U.S.C. 913]*	Amends the definition of rural area for programs authorized by the Rural Electrification Act to be the same as the definition in Section 3002 (28)(A)(i): any area other than a city or town with a population greater than 50,000 and the urbanized area contiguous and adjacent to such a city or town. *[Sec. 6101]*
Access to Broadband Telecommunications Services in Rural Area. Provides loan guarantees to establish broadband telecommunications infrastructure in rural areas. Subject to annual appropriations. *[7 U.S.C. 950bb]*	Reauthorizes funding for Access to Broadband Telecommunications Services in Rural Areas program at $50 million annually for 2008-2017, subject to appropriations. Amends Section 601 of the Rural Electrification Act to establish a grant component to the Broadband Loan Program. Establishes priorities for communities: 1)without a local service provider, 2) with populations of less than 20,000, 3) with a high proportion of low-income residents, and 4) experiencing significant out-migration. Also establishes a maximum grant limit of 50% of a project's development costs, but gives USDA the authority to increase the grant amount to 75% for remote communities and those with low-income residents. *[Sec. 6104]*
Expansion of 911 Access. Authorizes expanding the emergency telephone service of 911 in rural areas by using any funds otherwise made available for telephone loans for each of FY2008-FY2012. Section 315(d) of the Rural Electrification Act *[7 U.S.C. 940(e)d]*	Reauthorizes through FY2017. *[Sec. 6103]*
Distance Learning and Telemedicine Program. Provides grants to rural hospitals, clinics, schools, and libraries to develop and improve their telecommunications infrastructure. Section 233A of the Food, Agriculture, Conservation, and Trade Act of 1990. Authorizes funding of $100 million annually through FY2012, subject to appropriations. *[7 U.S.C. 950aaa]*	Reauthorizes funding for Distance Learning and Telemedicine Program at current level through 2017. *[Sec. 6201]*
No comparable provision.	Amends Subtitle E of Title VI of the 2002 farm bill (P.L. 101-171) to authorize a new Rural Energy Savings Program, which would provide 0% interest loans to eligible Rural Utilities Service borrowers to fund loans to qualified consumers to implement energy efficiency measures. *[Sec. 6402]*
Regional Development Authorities	
Delta Regional Authority. The Authority is an 8-state state-federal regional planning and development entity that provides loan and grant support for economic development projects in rural counties in the Mississippi Delta area. Authorizes $30 million annually for FY2008-2012 subject to appropriations. *[7 U.S.C. 2009aa et seq.]*	Reauthorizes funding through FY2017 for the Delta Regional Authority at the current level of $30 million annually, subject to appropriations. Also makes technical amendments to the operation of the Authority. Sections 3801 through 3814 of the ConAct. *[Sec. 6001]*

Current Law/Policy	Senate Agriculture Committee Farm Bill (S. 3240, as filed on May 24, 2012)
Northern Great Plains Regional Authority. Authorizes an economic development commission that develops regional plans and makes loans and grants for infrastructure and economic development in five Great Plains States. Authorizes $30 million annually for FY2008-2012, subject to appropriations. *[7 U.S.C. 2009bb et seq.]*	Reauthorizes funding through FY2017 for the Northern Great Plains Regional Authority at the current level of $30 million annually, subject to appropriations. Also makes technical amendments to the authority. Increases the cap on administrative expenses from 5% to 10%. Sections 3821 through 3835 of the ConAct. *[Sec. 6001]*

NOTE: See also **Title XII-Miscellaneous, Section 12205**, for changes made in the Senate bill to other regional commissions authorized by the 2008 farm bill. |

Title VII. Research, Extension, and Related Matters

Current Law/Policy	Senate Agriculture Committee Farm Bill (S. 3240, as filed on May 24, 2012)
Foundation for Food and Agricultural Research	
No comparable provision.	Provides mandatory funding of $100 million to establish the "Foundation for Food and Agriculture Research," a new nonprofit corporation designed to supplement USDA's basic and applied research activities. It will solicit and accept private donations to award grants for collaborative public/private partnerships with scientists at USDA and in academia, non-profits, and the private sector. The foundation will be exempt from taxation under section 501(a) of the Internal Revenue Code of 1986. [Sec. 7601]
National Agricultural Research, Extension, and Teaching Policy Act of 1977 (NARETPA), As Amended	
Authorizes the National Agricultural Research, Extension, Education, and Economics Advisory Board. The Board reviews and provides consultation on priorities for research, extension, education, and economics to the Secretary, land-grant colleges and universities, and Congress. [7 U.S.C. 3123]	Extends authority through FY2017 and adds "consult with industry groups" to the Board's list of duties. [Sec. 7101]
Amended by the Specialty Crops Competitiveness Act of 2004 (P.L. 108-465) to establish and allow USDA to appoint members to, a permanent specialty crops committee responsible for studying the scope and effectiveness of research, extension, and economics programs affecting the specialty crop industry. [7 U.S.C. 3123a]	Amends the requirements to provide for diversity of the specialty crops represented, and to ensure ongoing consultation with diverse sectors of the specialty crop industry. [Sec. 7102]
Authorizes a program to defray the school loans of veterinary medical school graduates who agree to serve for limited time periods in underserved areas. Funding subject to appropriations. [7 U.S.C. 3151a]	Authorizes an additional matching competitive grant program with qualified entities to develop, implement, and sustain veterinary services. Authorizes $10 million per year, subject to annual appropriations. [Sec. 7103]
Authorizes grants/fellowships to land grant colleges and universities for food and agricultural sciences education. Annual appropriations of $60 million authorized through FY2012. [7 U.S.C. 3152]	Reauthorizes at $40 million per year for FY2013-17, subject to appropriations. [Sec. 7104]
Authorizes USDA to enter into a wide variety of grants and other collaborative agreements with private and public educational institutions, corporations, and individuals to conduct independent research and public policy analysis on food and agriculture. Appropriations of such sums as necessary are authorized through FY2012. [7 U.S.C. 3155]	Reauthorizes at $5 million per year, subject to appropriations. Provides preference to policy research centers that have extensive databases, models, and demonstrated experience in providing Congress with agricultural projections and analysis at the farm, regional, national, and international levels. [Sec. 7105]
Authorizes USDA to make grants to Alaska Native-serving institutions to assist in carrying out education, applied research, and related community development programs. Annual appropriations of $10 million authorized through FY2012. [7 U.S.C. 3156]	Reauthorizes at $10 million per year for FY2013-17, subject to appropriations. [Sec. 7106]

Current Law/Policy	Senate Agriculture Committee Farm Bill (S. 3240, as filed on May 24, 2012)
Authorizes USDA to establish a national education program for disseminating results of food and human nutrition research performed or funded by USDA. Annual appropriations of $90 million authorized through FY2012. [7 U.S.C. 3175]	Reauthorizes at $90 million per year for FY2013-2017, subject to appropriations. [Sec. 7107]
Authorizes animal health and disease research. [7 U.S.C. 3195(a)]	Reauthorizes at $25 million per year for FY2013-2017, subject to appropriations. [Sec. 7108]
Authorizes annual appropriations of $25 million through FY2012 for NARETPA Grants to upgrade agricultural and food sciences facilities at 1890 land grant colleges, including Tuskegee University. [7 U.S.C. 3222b(b)] Annual appropriations of $8 million authorized through FY2012 for insular area land-grant institutions. [7 U.S.C. 3222b–2(d)]	Reauthorizes at $25 million per year and $8 million per year, respectively, for FY2013-2017, subject to appropriations. [Sections 7109 and 7110]
Authorizes grants to Hispanic-serving institutions to strengthen educational capacity. Annual appropriations of $40 million authorized through FY2012. [7 U.S.C. 3241]	Reauthorizes at $40 million per year for FY2013-2017, subject to appropriations. [Sec. 7111]
Authorizes competitive grants for international agricultural science and education programs. Appropriations of such sums as necessary are authorized through FY2012. [7 U.S.C. 3292b]	Reauthorizes at $5 million per year for FY2013-2017, subject to appropriations. [Sec. 7112]
Authorizes university agricultural research. Appropriations of such sums as necessary are authorized through FY2012. [7 U.S.C. 3311]	Reauthorizes for FY2013-2017, subject to appropriations. [Sec. 7113]
Authorizes agricultural extension activities. Appropriations of such sums as necessary are authorized through FY2012. [7 U.S.C. 3312]	Reauthorizes for FY2013-2017, subject to appropriations. [Sec. 7114]
Authorizes research on supplemental and alternative crops, subject to appropriations. [7 U.S.C. 3319d]	Reauthorizes at $1 million per year for FY2013-2017, subject to appropriations, and amends so that only competitive grants can be awarded. [Sec. 7115]
Authorizes competitive grants to non-land grant colleges of agriculture. Appropriations of such sums as necessary are authorized through FY2012. [7 U.S.C. 3319i(b)]	Reauthorizes for FY2013-2017, subject to appropriations. [Sec. 7116]
Authorizes grants for a cooperative research and extension program to encourage the development, management, and production of aquatic food species. [7 U.S.C. 3322(b)]	Reauthorizes at $5 million per year for FY2013-2017, subject to appropriations, and amends so that only competitive grants can be awarded. [Sec. 7117]
Authorizes rangeland research. Annual appropriations of $10 million authorized through FY2012. [7 U.S.C. 3336(a)]	Reauthorizes at $2 million per year for FY2013-2017, subject to appropriations. [Sec. 7118]
Authorizes biosecurity planning/response. Appropriations of such sums as necessary are authorized through FY2012. [7 U.S.C. 3351(a)]	Reauthorizes at $20 million per year for FY2013-2017, subject to appropriations. [Sec. 7119]

Current Law/Policy	Senate Agriculture Committee Farm Bill (S. 3240, as filed on May 24, 2012)
Authorizes resident instruction & distance education grants for insular area institutions of higher education. Appropriations of such sums as necessary are authorized through FY2012. *[7 U.S.C. 3362(a)]*	Reauthorizes at $2 million per year for FY2013-2017, subject to appropriations, and amends so that only competitive grants can be awarded. *[Sec. 7120]*
Food, Agriculture, Conservation, and Trade Act of 1990, As Amended	
Provides for research on best utilization of biological applications. Annual appropriations of $40 million authorized. *[7 U.S.C. 5814]*	Reauthorizes at $40 million per year for FY2013-2017, subject to appropriations. *[Sec. 7201]*
Provides for a research and education program on integrated resource management and integrated crop management. Annual appropriations of $20 million authorized. *[7 U.S.C. 5821]*	Reauthorizes at $20 million per year for FY2013-2017, subject to appropriations. *[Sec. 7202]*
Provides for information on sustainable agriculture. Appropriations of such sums as necessary are authorized. *[7 U.S.C. 5831]* Education/training for Cooperative Extension Service agents and other professionals is also provided. Annual appropriations of $20 million authorized. *[7 U.S.C. 5832]*	For FY2013-17, reauthorizes at such sums as necessary *[Sec. 7203]* and $20 million per year *[Sec. 7204]*, subject to appropriations.
Provides for a national genetics resources program. Appropriations of such sums as necessary are authorized through FY2012. *[7 U.S.C. 5844(b)]*	Reauthorizes at $1 million per year for FY2013-2017, subject to appropriations. *[Sec. 7205]*
Provides for a national agricultural weather information system. Annual appropriations of $5 million authorized through FY2012. *[7 U.S.C. 5855(c)]*	Reauthorizes at $1 million per year for FY2013-2017, subject to appropriations. *[Sec. 7206]*
Provides for research and extension on a number of high-priority topics, including aflatoxin, prickly pears, and deer tick ecology. Annual appropriations of $10 million authorized through FY2012. *[7 U.S.C. 5925]*	Reauthorizes at $25 million per year for FY2013-2017, subject to appropriations. Adds a new pulse crop health and extension initiative to address the critical needs of the pulse crop industry. *[Sec. 7207]*
Establishes the Organic Agriculture Research and Extension Initiative (OREI), providing grants to facilitate the development of organic agriculture production and processing. Provides mandatory CCC funds of $18 million (FY2009) and $20 million annually (FY2010-FY2012), and authorizes annual appropriations of $25 million (FY2009-FY2012). *[7 U.S.C. 5925b]*	Reauthorizes OREI with some program changes. Provides CCC funds of $16 million (FY2013-FY2017) and extends authority for appropriated funding of $25 million through FY2017. *[Sec. 7208]*
Authorizes competitive research and extension grants for improving the farm business management knowledge and skills of agricultural producers. Appropriations of such sums as necessary are authorized. *[7 U.S.C. 5925f(d)]*	Reauthorizes at $5 million per year for FY2013-2017, subject to appropriations. *[Sec. 7209]*
Authorizes regional centers of excellence. Appropriations of such sums as necessary are authorized through FY2012. *[7 U.S.C. 5925]*	Reauthorizes at $10 million per year for FY2013-2017, subject to appropriations. *[Sec. 7210]*
Authorizes an assistive technology program for farmers with disabilities. Annual appropriations of $6 million authorized through FY2012. *[7 U.S.C. 5933(c)(1)]*	Reauthorizes at $5 million per year for FY2013-2017, subject to appropriations. *[Sec. 7211]*
Authorizes National Rural Information Center Clearinghouse. Annual appropriations of $500,000 authorized through FY2012. *[7 U.S.C. 3125b(e)]*	Reauthorizes at $500,000 per year for FY2013-2017, subject to appropriations. *[Sec. 7212]*

Current Law/Policy	Senate Agriculture Committee Farm Bill (S. 3240), As Amended
Agriculture Research, Extension, and Education Reform Act of 1998 (AREERA)	**As Amended**
USDA establishes procedures that provide for scientific peer review of agricultural research grants administered, on a competitive basis, by its National Institute of Food and Agriculture. [7 U.S.C. 7613]	Amends law to emphasize that "relevance" of the underlying research and extension programs to the affected industry shall be considered in evaluating grant applications. [Sec. 7301]
Section 406, as amended, establishes the "Integrated Research, Education, And Extension Competitive Grants Program." Included is the Organic Transitions Program (ORG), which funds research, extension, and education programs to improve the competitiveness of organic producers and producers transitioning to organic practices. Appropriations of such sums as necessary are authorized through FY2012. [7 U.S.C. 7626]	Reauthorizes program and extends authority to appropriate funds for FY2013-2017. [Sec. 7302]
Section 408(e) authorizes research on diseases of wheat, triticale, and barley caused by Fusarium graminearum or by Tilletia indica. Appropriations of such sums as necessary are authorized through FY2012. [7 U.S.C.7628(e)]	Reauthorizes program at $10 million per year for FY2013-2017, subject to appropriations. [Sec. 7303]
Section 410(d) authorizes grants for youth organizations. Appropriations of such sums as necessary are authorized through FY2012. [7 U.S.C.7630(d)]	Reauthorizes program at $3 million per year for FY2013-2017, subject to appropriations. [Sec. 7304]
Section 7311 of the 2008 farm bill amended the AREERA to establish the Specialty Crop Research Initiative (SCRI), providing mandatory CCC funds of $30 million (FY2008) and $50 million annually (FY2009-FY2012), plus authorizes $100 million annually (FY2008-FY2012), subject to appropriations. [7 U.S.C. 7632]	Reauthorizes SCRI. Provides mandatory CCC funds of $25 million (FY2013); $30 million annually (FY2014-FY2015); $65 million (FY2016); and $50 million (FY2017 and each fiscal year thereafter). Extends authority to appropriate funds through FY2017. Requires USDA consult with the specialty crops committee during the peer and merit review process. [Sec. 7305]
Sec. 604 of AREERA authorizes the Food Animal Residue Avoidance Database. Appropriations of such sums as necessary are authorized through FY2012. [7 U.S.C. 7642]	Reauthorizes program and extends authority to appropriate funds for FY2013-2017. [Sec. 7306]
AREERA establishes the Office of Pest Management Policy to coordinate USDA's policies and activities related to pesticides and pest management tools. Authorizes appropriations of such sums as necessary through FY2012. [7 U.S.C. 7653]	Reauthorizes appropriations of $3 million annually (FY2013- FY2017). [Section 7307] Amends Title VI of AREERA [7 U.S.C. 7651 et seq.] to establish four "Regional Integrated Pest Management Centers" (located in the north central, northeastern, southern, and western regions) to provide research and extension programs, outreach, and response to information needs, among other purposes. [Sec. 7308]
Authorities in Other Laws	
Provides for development of critical agricultural materials. Appropriations of such sums as necessary are authorized through FY2012. [7 U.S.C. 178n]	Reauthorizes at $2 million per year for FY2013-2017, subject to appropriations. [Sec. 7401]
1994 institutions (tribally controlled colleges) are defined. [7 U.S.C. 301]	Updates the list of institutions. Makes changes in grant process. [Sec. 7402]
Authorizes funding for costs of agricultural research facilities (experiment stations) under the Research Facilities Act. Appropriations of such sums as necessary are authorized through FY2012. [7 U.S.C. 390d(a)]	Extends authority to appropriate funds through FY2017. [Sec. 7403]

Current Law/Policy	Senate Agriculture Committee Farm Bill (S. 3240, as filed on May 24, 2012)
The Agriculture and Food Research Initiative (AFRI) makes competitive grants for fundamental and applied research, and for purchasing research equipment. Authorized funding at $700 million annually from FY2008 through FY2012, subject to appropriations. [7 U.S.C. 450i]	Reauthorizes at $700 million per year for AFRI through FY2017. Directs USDA to streamline the competitive grant process for eligible institutions with limited resources. [Sec. 7404]
USDA operates a National Agricultural Library to serve as the primary agricultural information resource of the United States. [7 U.S.C. 3125a]	Reauthorizes through FY2017 the authority to lease property of the Beltsville Agricultural Research Center or the Library to any individual or entity. [Sec. 7405]
The Renewable Resources Extension Act of 1978 (P.L. 95-306) authorizes educational and technical aid via state extension agencies and eligible universities and colleges. Authorizes annual appropriations of $30 million (FY2009-FY2012). [16 U.S.C. 1671-1676]	Reauthorizes at $30 million per year for FY2013-2017, subject to appropriations. [Sec. 7406]
Section 10 of the National Aquaculture Act of 1980 establishes USDA as the lead Federal agency for coordinating and disseminating national aquaculture information. Authorizes annual appropriations of $3 million through FY2012. [16 U.S.C. 2801]	Extends authority to appropriate funds through FY2017. [Sec. 7407]
Establishes the Beginning Farmer and Rancher Development Program; provides training, education, outreach/technical assistance initiatives. Provides mandatory CCC funds of $18 million (FY2009) and $19 million annually (FY2010-FY2012), plus authorizes $30 million annually (FY2008-FY2012), subject to appropriations. [7 U.S.C. 3319f]	Provides for a one-time mandatory funding of $50 million in FY2013 (to be available until expended) and extends authority to appropriate funds through FY2017. List of groups receiving funding set-aside (not less than 25% of total) is expanded to include military veterans. [Sec. 7408]
Food, Conservation, and Energy Act of 2008	
Establishes a communication center to prepare for an agricultural disease emergency or threat to agricultural biosecurity. Appropriations of such sums as necessary are authorized for FY2008 through FY2012. [7 U.S.C. 8912]	Reauthorizes programs at $2 million per year for FY2013-2017, subject to appropriations. [Sec. 7501]
Provides assistance to build local capacity in agricultural biosecurity planning, preparedness, and response. Appropriations of such sums as necessary are authorized for FY2008 through FY2012. [7 U.S.C. 8913]	Reauthorizes at $15 million per year for FY2013-2017, subject to appropriations. [Sec. 7502]
Establishes a competitive grant program to promote the development of teaching programs in disciplines closely allied to the food and agriculture system to increase the number of trained individuals with an expertise in agricultural biosecurity. Appropriations of such sums as necessary are authorized for FY2008 through FY2012. [7 U.S.C. 8922(e)]	Reauthorizes at $5 million per year for FY2013-2017, subject to appropriations. [Sec. 7504]
Establishes a competitive grant program to encourage basic and applied research and the development of qualified agricultural countermeasures to respond to an outbreak of plant disease. Annual appropriations of $50 million are authorized for FY2008 through FY2012. [7 U.S.C. 8921(b)]	Reauthorizes program at $15 million per year for FY2013-2017, subject to appropriations.. [Sec. 7503]

Current Law/Policy	Senate Agriculture Committee Farm Bill (S. 3240, as filed on May 24, 2012)
Prohibits the Grazinglands Research Laboratory at El Reno, Oklahoma from being declared excess or surplus Federal property.	Reauthorizes provision through FY2017. [Sec. 7511]
In the annual budget process, the President is required to submit to Congress a single budget line item reflecting the total amount requested by the President for funding for research, education, and extension activities of the Research, Education, and Economics mission area of USDA for each fiscal year and for the preceding 5 years. [7 U.S.C. 7614c]	Requires the budget submission to include sufficient information for Congress to thoroughly evaluate and approve future spending plans with regard to extramural competitive grants programs and intramural research spending. New language is added to create transparency and accountability for USDA research programs. [Sec. 7512]
Establishes a program of research relating to natural products, including products from plant, marine, and microbial sources. Appropriations of such sums as necessary are authorized for FY2008 through FY2012. [7 U.S.C. 5937]	Reauthorizes at $7 million per year for FY2013-2017, subject to appropriations. [Sec. 7513]
Establishes bioenergy research programs through "sun" grants to land grant institutions and five regional centers. The research is to enhance national energy security through the development, distribution, and implementation of biobased energy technologies. Annual appropriations of $75 million (FY2008-FY2012) are authorized [7 U.S.C. 8114]	Consolidates and amends the Sun Grant Program to expand input from other appropriate federal agencies and replace authority for gasification research with bioproducts research. Makes program competitive by removing designation of certain universities as regional centers. Reauthorizes at $75 million per year for FY2013-2017, subject to appropriations. [Sec. 7514]

Title VIII. Forestry

Current Law/Policy	Senate Agriculture Committee Farm Bill (S. 3240, as filed on May 24, 2012)
Program Repeal	
Sec. 4 of the Cooperative Forestry Assistance Act of 1978 (CFAA, P.L. 95-313), as amended, authorizes and establishes the Forest Land Enhancement Program (FLEP) between FY2002-FY2008. The program was not reauthorized in the 2008 farm bill. [*16 U.S.C. 2301*]	Repeals FLEP, effective October 1, 2012. [*Sec. 8001*]
Sec. 6 of the CFAA, as amended, authorizes and establishes the Watershed Forestry Assistance Program (WFAP) between FY2004-FY2008. Funding has never been appropriated. [*16 U.S.C. 2301b*]	Repeals WFAP, effective October 1, 2012. [*Sec. 8002*]
Sec. 18 of the CFAA, as amended, authorizes and establishes the Cooperative National Forest Products Marketing Program between FY1988-FY1991. Since FY1993, funding is appropriated through the Economic Action Program (EAP) administered by the U.S. Forest Service. [*16 U.S.C. 2112*]	Repeals the Cooperative National Forest Products Marketing Program, effective October 1, 2012. [*Sec. 8003*]
S. 8402 of the 2008 farm bill, as amended, authorizes the Hispanic-serving institution agricultural land national resources leadership program to provide undergraduate forestry scholarships. Funding has never been appropriated. [*16 U.S.C. 1649a*]	Repeals the Hispanic-serving institution agricultural land national resources leadership program, effective October 1, 2012. [*Sec. 8004*]
Sec. 303 of the Healthy Forest Restoration Act of 2003 (HFRA, P.L. 108-148), as amended, authorizes and establishes the Tribal watershed forestry assistance program between FY2004-FY2008. Funding has never been appropriated. [*16. U.S.C. 6542*]	Repeals the Tribal watershed forestry assistance program, effective October 1, 2012. [*Sec. 8005*]
Reauthorization of Forestry-Related Programs	
Sec. 2A(f)(1) of the CFAA, as amended, authorizes up to $10 million in annual appropriations between FY2008-FY2012 to carry out the state-wide assessment and strategies for forest resources. [*16 U.S.C. 2101a(f)(1)*]	Reauthorizes funding to carry out the state-wide assessment and strategies for forest resources at $10 million annually through FY2017. [*Sec. 8101*]
Sec. 5(h) of the CFAA, as amended, permanently authorizes such sums as necessary to be appropriated each fiscal year after 1996, to carry out the Forest Stewardship Program (FSP). FSP was created to improve timber production and environmental protection on nonfederal forest lands and received average annual appropriations of approximately $30 million from FY2008-FY2012. [*16 U.S.C 2103a(h)*]	Eliminates permanent authority to receive annual appropriations of such sums as necessary, instead authorized to receive $50 million annually through for FY2013-FY2017, subject to appropriations. [*Sec. 8102*]
Sec. 7 of the CFAA, as amended, permanently authorizes such sums as necessary to be appropriated to carry out the Forest Legacy Program (FLP). FLP was created to protect forests that might soon be cleared for non-forest uses and received average annual appropriations of approximately $58 million from FY2008-FY2012. [*16 U.S.C. 2103c*]	Eliminates permanent authority to receive annual appropriations of such sums as necessary, instead authorized to receive $200 million annually through for FY2013-FY2017, subject to appropriations. Provides flexibility for using other funding sources. [*Sec. 8103*]

Comparison of Senate Agriculture Committee 2012 Farm Bill (S. 3240) with Current Law

Current Law/Policy	Senate Agriculture Committee Farm Bill (S. 3240, as filed on May 24, 2012)
Sec. 7a of the CFAA, as amended, permanently authorizes such sums as necessary to be appropriated to carry out the Community Forest and Open Space Conservation program. The program provides financial assistance to local governments, tribes, and nonprofit organizations for preventing the conversion of forestland to non-forest uses. Appropriations between FY2010-FY2012 for this program were less than $2 million annually. *[16 U.S.C. 2103d]*	Eliminates permanent authority to receive annual appropriations of such sums as necessary, instead authorized to receive $50 million annually through for FY2013-FY2017, subject to appropriations. *[Sec. 8104]*
Sec. 9i of the CFAA, as amended, permanently authorizes such sums as necessary to be appropriated to carry out urban and community forestry assistance. The program was created to expand awareness and use of urban tree cover and received an average annual appropriations of approximately $30 million from FY2008-FY2012. *[16 U.S.C. 2105i]*	Eliminates permanent authority to receive annual appropriations of such sums as necessary, instead authorized to receive $50 million annually through for FY2013-FY2017, subject to appropriations. *[Sec. 8105]*
Sec. 2371(d)(2) of the Food, Agriculture, Conservation, and Trade Act of 1990 (P.L. 101-624, 1990 farm bill), as amended, authorizes appropriations of $5 million annually through FY2012 to carry out the rural revitalization technologies program. *[7 U.S.C. 6601(d)(2)]*	Reauthorizes funding to carry out the rural revitalization technologies program at $5 million annually through FY2017 subject to appropriations. *[Sec. 8201]*
Sec. 2405 of the Global Climate Change Prevention Act of 1990 (within the 1990 farm bill), as amended, authorizes such sums as necessary to be appropriated to administer the Office of International Forestry until FY2012. The office received an average annual appropriations of approximately $7.5 million from FY2008-FY2012. *[7 U.S.C. 6704]*	Eliminates authority to receive such sums as necessary, instead reauthorizes the Office of International Forestry at $10 million annually for FY2013-FY2017, subject to appropriations. *[Sec. 8202]*
Sec. 401 of the HFRA, as amended, lists insects and diseases identified by Congress as adversely affecting forest health. *[16 U.S.C. 6551(a)]*	Adds the mountain pine beetle to the list of insect infestations and diseases identified by Congress. *[Sec. 8203(a)]*
No comparable provision.	Requires USDA to designate treatment areas in at least one national forest in each state, if requested by the Governor of the state, where there is declining forest health from insect or disease infestation. Authorizes appropriations of $100 million annually through FY2017. New Sec. 405 of the HFRA *[Sec. 8203(b)]*
Sec. 406 of the HFRA, as amended, authorizes such sums as necessary to be appropriated to carry out an insect and disease assessment program though FY2008. *[16 U.S.C. 6556]*	Reauthorizes funding to carry out the assessment program at such sums as necessary annually through FY2017, subject to appropriations. Amended Sec. 407. *[Sec. 8203(c)]*
Sec. 508 of the HFRA, as amended, authorizes the Healthy Forests Reserve Program (HFRP) to receive $9.75 million of mandatory funding annually through FY2012. *[16 U.S.C. 3578]*	Eliminates mandatory funding authority and replaces with authorization to receive appropriations of $9.75 million annually through FY2017. Provides flexibility for funding technical assistance. *[Sec. 8204]*

Current Law/Policy	Senate Agriculture Committee Farm Bill (S. 3240, as filed on May 24, 2012)
Sec. 347 of the Department of the Interior and Related Agencies Appropriations Act of 1999 (P.L. 105-277), as amended, authorizes the Forest Service and Bureau of Land Management to enter into stewardship end-result contracting projects (stewardship contracts) to enter into contracts or agreements for services to achieve land management goals and meet local and rural community needs. Authority expires September 30, 2013. *[16 U.S.C. 2104, note]*	Repeals current authority and adds similar provisions to create a new Sec. 602 of the HFRA, as amended. Authorizes stewardship contracts, of 5-10 years, to achieve land management goals. Includes performance, monitoring, evaluation, and reporting requirements. *[Sec. 8205]*
Miscellaneous Provisions	
Sec. 502(e)(3) of the HFRA, as amended, authorizes the enrollment of acreage owned by Indian tribes into HFRP through 30-year contracts, 10-year cost-share agreements, or any combination thereof. *[16 U.S.C. 6572(e)(3)]*	Adds a definition of 'acreage owned by Indian tribes.' Enrollment options are unchanged. *[Sec. 8206]*
Sec. 4 of the McIntire-Stennis Cooperative Forestry Act (P.L. 87-788), as amended, establishes funding requirements for college and university forestry-related research. *[16 U.S.C. 582a-3]*	Waives the matching requirements for 1890 Institutions for allocations below $200,000. *[Sec. 8301(a)]*
Sec. 8 of the McIntire-Stennis Cooperative Forestry Act, as amended, defines 'states' as including Puerto Rico, the Virgin Islands, and Guam. *[16 U.S.C. 582a-7]*	Adds Federated States of Micronesia, American Samoa, and the Northern Mariana Islands to the definition of 'state.' *[Sec. 8301(b)]*
Sec. 3(e) of the Forest and Rangeland Renewable Resources Research Act of 1978 (P.L. 95-307), as amended, requires USDA to establish a program to inventory and analyze public and private forests and their resources. *[16 U.S.C. 1642(e)]*	Requires USDA to revise the strategic plan for forest inventory and analysis and report revisions to congress. *[Sec. 8302]*

Title IX. Energy

Current Law/Policy	Senate Agriculture Committee Farm Bill (S. 3240, as filed on May 24, 2012)
Definitions	
Advanced Biofuel: Fuel derived from renewable biomass other than corn kernel starch. Includes biofuel derived from sugar and starch other than corn kernel starch, renewable biodiesel, biogas produced from organic matter, as well as other fuels (e.g., home heating fuels, and aviation and jet fuels) from cellulosic biomass (including organic waste material). *[7 U.S.C. 8101(3)]*	Same as current law. *[Sec. 9001]*
Biobased Product: A commercial or industrial product (i.e., intermediate, feedstock, or end product) composed in whole or in part of biological products including renewable agricultural and forestry materials. *[7 U.S.C. 8101(4)]*	Same as current law. *[Sec. 9001]*
Biofuel: A fuel derived from renewable biomass. *[7 U.S.C. 8101(5)]*	Same as current law. *[Sec. 9001]*
Biomass Conversion Facility: A facility that converts renewable biomass into heat, power, biobased products, or advanced biofuels. *[7 U.S.C. 8101(6)]*	Same as current law. *[Sec. 9001]*
Biorefinery: A facility (including equipment and processes) that converts renewable biomass into biofuels and biobased products, and may produce electricity. *[7 U.S.C. 8101(7)]*	Same as current law. *[Sec. 9001]*
Renewable Biomass: Includes- (A) materials, pre-commercial thinnings, or invasive species from National Forest System land and public lands that are: byproducts of designated preventive treatments (removed to reduce hazardous fuels, to reduce or to contain disease or insect infestation, or to restore ecosystem health), not used for higher value products, and harvested in accordance with applicable law and land management plans and requirements for old-growth maintenance, restoration, and management and large-tree retention, or (B) any organic matter available on a recurring basis from non-federal or Indian land including: renewable plant material (including agricultural commodities, plants and trees, and algae) and waste material (including crop residue, vegetative waste, wood waste and residues, animal waste and byproducts, and food and yard waste). *[7 U.S.C. 8101(12)]*	Same as current law. *[Sec. 9001]*
Renewable Energy: Energy derived from a wind, solar, renewable biomass, ocean (including tidal, wave, current, and thermal), geothermal, or hydroelectric source. *[7 U.S.C. 8101(13)]*	Same as current law. *[Sec. 9001]*
No comparable definition.	**Renewable Chemical:** A monomer, polymer, plastic, formulated product, or chemical substance produced from renewable biomass. *[Sec. 9001]*

Current Law/Policy	Senate Agriculture Committee Farm Bill (S. 3240, as filed on May 24, 2012)
Authorized Programs	
Biobased Markets Program: Extended by the 2008 farm bill. Requires federal agencies to purchase products with maximum biobased content subject to availability and flexibility and performance standards. Minimum biobased content standards applied to federal contracts on case-by-case basis. Continued voluntary labeling. Authorized mandatory funding of $1 million for FY2008 and $2 million annually for FY2009-FY2012. Authorized to be appropriated $2 million annually for FY2009-FY2012 for testing and labeling. *[7 U.S.C. 8102]*	Extends the Biobased Markets Program through FY2017 subject to additional reporting requirements by procuring federal agencies. Adds an outreach, education, and promotion component to increase awareness of biobased products. Mandates study (and report) by USDA to assess economic impact of biobased product industry, due 180 days after enactment. Encourages expedited review and approval of forest-related biobased products. Authorizes mandatory funding of $3 million annually for FY2013-FY2017. Authorizes to be appropriated $2 million annually for FY2013-FY2017. *[Sec. 9002]*
Biorefinery Assistance Program: Established by the 2008 farm bill. Assists in development of new and emerging technologies for advanced biofuels by providing competitive grants (up to 30% of total project costs) and loan guarantees (limited to $250 million or 80% of project cost) for construction and/or retrofitting of demonstration-scale biorefineries to demonstrate the commercial viability of one or more processes for converting renewable biomass to advanced biofuels. Provided mandatory funding of $75 million in FY2009 and $245 million in FY2010, available until expended, for loan guarantees. Authorized to be appropriated $150 million annually for FY2009-12 for grants. *[7 U.S.C. 8103]*	**Biorefinery, Renewable Chemical, and Biobased Product Manufacturing Assistance Program:** Extends and expands the program to include renewable chemical and biobased product manufacturing. Authorized mandatory funding of $100 million for FY2013 and $58 million each for FY2014-FY2015, but not more than $25 million of FY2013-FY2015 may be used to promote biobased product manufacturing. Authorized to be appropriated $150 million annually for FY2013-FY2017. *[Sec. 9003]*
Repowering Assistance Program: Established by the 2008 farm bill. Provides funds to reduce or eliminate the use of fossil fuels for processing or power in biorefineries in existence at enactment. Not more than 5% of funds are available to eligible producers with a refining capacity exceeding 150 million gallons of advanced biofuel per year. Provided mandatory CCC funding of $35 million for FY2009, available until expended. Authorized to be appropriated $15 million annually for FY2009-12. *[7 U.S.C. 8104]*	Repeals the Repowering Assistance Program and transfers the remaining funds (of approximately $25 million to remain available until expended) to the Rural Energy for America Program (REAP). *[Sec. 9004]*
Bioenergy Program for Advanced Biofuels: Established by the 2008 farm bill. Provides payments to producers to support and expand production of advanced biofuels by entering into contracts to pay producers for production of eligible advanced biofuels. Provided mandatory funding of $55 million (FY2009), $55 million (FY2010), $85 million (FY2011), and $105 million (FY2012). Authorized to be appropriated $25 million annually (FY2009-12) *[7 U.S.C. 8105]*	Extends the Bioenergy Program for Advanced Biofuels Program through FY2017. Authorizes to be appropriated $20 million annually for FY2013-FY2017. *[Sec. 9005]*
Biodiesel Fuel Education Program: Extended by the 2008 farm bill. Awards competitive grants to nonprofit organizations that educate fleet operators and the public on biodiesel benefits. Provided mandatory CCC funding of $1 million annually (FY2008-FY2012). *[7 U.S.C. 8106]*	Extends the the Biodiesel Fuel Education Program through FY2017. Authorizes mandatory funding of $1 million annually for FY2013-FY2017. Authorizes to be appropriated $1 million annually for FY2013-FY2017. *[Sec. 9006]*

Current Law/Policy	Senate Agriculture Committee Farm Bill (S. 3240, as filed on May 24, 2012)
Rural Energy for America Program (REAP): Established by the 2008 farm bill. Provides financial assistance of grants, guaranteed loans, and combined grants and guaranteed loans for the development and construction of renewable energy systems (RES) and for energy efficiency improvement (EEI) projects (eligible entities include rural small businesses and agricultural producers); grants for conducting energy audits and for conducting renewable energy development assistance (eligible entities include state, tribe, or local governments, land-grant colleges and universities, rural electric cooperatives, and public power entities); and grants for conducting RES feasibility studies (eligible entities include rural small businesses and agricultural producers). Grants are limited to $500,000 for RES and $250,000 for EEI activities up to 25% of the cost of the RES or EEI activity. Loan guarantees are limited to a max of $25 million and a min of $5,000 up to 75% of the cost of a funded activity. Provides mandatory funds: $55 million (FY2009), $60 million (FY2010), $70 million (FY2011), and $70 million (FY2012). Authorizes $25 million annually, subject to appropriations (FY2009-FY2012). *[7 U.S.C. 8107]*	Extends REAP through FY2017. Repeals the use of REAP funds for feasibility studies. Grants are limited to the lesser of $500,000 or 25% of the cost of the RES or EEI activity, while loan guarantees are limited to $25 million, and the combined grant and loan guarantee may not exceed 75% of the cost of a funded activity. Adds a 3-tiered application process with separate application processes for grants and loan guarantees for RES and EEI projects based on the project cost: tier-1 for projects ≤ $80,000; tier-2 for $80,000 < projects < $200,000; and tier-3 for projects > $200,000. Authorizes mandatory funding of $48.2 million annually for FY2013-FY2017. Authorizes to be appropriated $20 million annually for FY2013-FY2017. *[Sec. 9007]*
Biomass Research & Development Initiative (BRDI): Created originally under the Biomass Research & Development Act of 2000 [P.L. 106-224], and extended by the 2008 farm bill. Provides competitive funding as grants, contracts, and financial assistance for research, development, and demonstration of technologies and processes leading to commercial production of biofuels and biobased products. Provides for coordination between USDA and DOE work related to biofuels and biobased products research and development programs through the Biomass Research and Development Board. Provides mandatory funding: $20 million (FY2009), $28 million (FY2010), $30 million (FY1022), and $40 million (FY2012). Authorizes to be appropriated $35 million annually (FY2009-FY2012). *[7 U.S.C. 8108]*	Extends BRDI through FY2017. Authorizes mandatory funding of $26 million annually for FY2013-FY2017. Authorizes to be appropriated $30 million annually for FY2013-FY2017. *[Sec. 9008]*
Rural Energy Self-Sufficiency Initiative: Established by amended section 9009 [Sec. 9001] of the 2008 farm bill. Provides cost-share (up to 50%) grants for rural communities to assess energy systems and to make improvements. Authorizes to be appropriated $5 million annually (FY2009-FY2012); however, no funds were ever appropriated and no rules were ever promulgated. *[7 U.S.C. 8109]*	No comparable provision.
Feedstock Flexibility Program: Established by the 2008 farm bill. Authorizes use of CCC funds (such sums as necessary) to purchase sugar (intended for food use but deemed to be in surplus) for resale as a biomass feedstock to produce bioenergy. USDA would implement the program only in those years where purchases are determined to be necessary to ensure that the sugar program operates at no cost to the federal government. *[7 U.S.C. 8110]*	Extends the Feed Stock Flexibility Program through FY2017. *[Sec. 9009]*

Current Law/Policy	Senate Agriculture Committee Farm Bill (S. 3240, as filed on May 24, 2012)
Biomass Crop Assistance Program (BCAP): Established by the 2008 farm bill. Provides financial assistance to owners and operators of agricultural land and non-industrial private forest land who wish to establish, produce, and deliver biomass feedstocks under two categories of assistance: (A) establishment and annual payments are provided under contract between USDA and participating producers including a one-time payment of up to 75% of cost of establishment for perennial crops, and annual payments (i.e., rental rates based on a set of criteria) of up to 5 years for non-woody and 15 years for woody perennial biomass crops, and (B) matching payments at a rate of $1 per ton provided up to $45 per ton for a period of 2 years to help eligible material owners with collection, harvest, storage, and transportation (CHST) of eligible material for use in a qualified biomass conversion facility. Eligible material excludes Title I crops, animal waste and byproducts, food and yard waste, and algae. Provides mandatory CCC funding of such sums as necessary annually for FY2008-FY2012. *[7 U.S.C. 8111]*	Extends BCAP through FY2017. Excludes algae as an eligible crop; adds land enrolled in the agricultural conservation easement program as eligible land, includes crop residue from crops receiving Title I payments as eligible material, but extends exclusion to any whole grain from a Title I crop, as well as bagasse. One-time establishment payments are limited to no more than 50% of cost of establishment, not to exceed $500 per acre ($750 per acre for socially disadvantaged farmers or ranchers). CHST matching payments may not exceed $20 per dry ton but are available for a period of 4 years. Not later than 4 years after enactment, USDA shall submit a report on best practice data and information gathered from participants. Authorizes mandatory funding of $38.6 million annually for FY2013-FY2017. Not less than 10%, nor more than 50% ,of funding may be used for CHST. *[Sec. 9010]*
Forest Biomass for Energy Program: Established by the 2008 farm bill. Requires the Forest Service to conduct a competitive research and development program to encourage use of forest biomass for energy. Authorized to be appropriated $15 million annually (FY2009-FY2012). *[7 U.S.C. 8112]*	Repeals the Forest Biomass for Energy Program. *[Sec. 9011]*
Community Wood Energy Program: Established by the 2008 farm bill. Provides grants of up to $50,000 for up to 50% of the cost for communities to plan and install wood energy systems in public buildings. The energy system acquired with grant funds shall not exceed an output of 50,000,000 Btu per hour for heating and 2 megawatts for electric power production. Authorized to be appropriated $5 million annually (FY2009-FY12). *[7 U.S.C. 8113]*	Extends the Community Wood Energy Program through FY2017. Authorizes to be appropriated $5 million annually for FY2013-FY2017. *[Sec. 9012]*

Title X. Horticulture
(unless otherwise specified)

Current Law/Policy	Senate Agriculture Committee Farm Bill (S. 3240, as filed on May 24, 2012)
Marketing and Promotion, and Trade	
The Specialty Crops Competitiveness Act of 2004 (P.L. 108-465), as amended by the 2008 farm bill, authorized block grants to states to support projects in marketing, research, pest management, and food safety, among other purposes. Current mandatory CCC funding is $55 million annually (FY2010-FY2012). *[7 U.S.C. 1621 note]*	Reauthorizes program through FY2017. Increases mandatory funding to $70 million annually (FY2013 through FY2017), which would also raise the minimum grant amount received by each state/territory. Of the funds provided, allows for multistate project grants involving food safety, plant pests and disease, crop-specific projects addressing common issues, and any other area as determined by USDA, with increased funding starting at $1 million (FY2013) to $5 million. Establishes limits on use of funding for program administration. *[Sec. 10008]* Changes effective October 1, 2012. *[Sec. 10011]*
The Farmer-to-Consumer Direct Marketing Act (P.L. 94-463), as amended, originally authorized the Farmers' Market Promotion Program (FMPP) to promote farmers' markets, roadside stands, community-supported agriculture programs, agri-tourism activities, and other direct producer-to-consumer market opportunities. Authorized annual appropriations for grants to local governments and nonprofit organizations. Current mandatory CCC funding is $10 million annually (FY2011-FY2012). *[7 U.S.C. 3005]*	Reauthorizes the current program, but changes the scope and name of the program to the "Farmers Market and Local Food Promotion Program." Expands the program to include local and regional food enterprises that process, distribute, aggregate, store, and market locally or regionally produced food products, designating 50% of available funds for this purpose. Increases mandatory funding to $20 million annually (FY2013 through FY2017). Establishes limits on use of funding for program administration. *[Sec. 10003]* Changes effective October 1, 2012. *[Sec. 10011]*
	Note: Another related provision is in Title IV (Nutrition, the Seniors Farmers' Market Nutrition Program). [Sec. 4202].
Section 10403 of the 2008 farm bill authorized grants to various public and private entities to improve transporting specialty crops to markets. Provided for "appropriations of such sums as necessary."	Repeals authorization under section 10403 of the 2008 farm bill. *[Section 10002]* Changes effective October 1, 2012. *[Sec. 10011]*
See also Title III (Trade) for reauthorization of Technical Assistance for Specialty Crops (TASC) *[7 U.S.C. 5680]* and the Market Access Program (MAP) *[7 U.S.C. 5623]*	See Title III – Trade. *[Sec. 3205]* and *[Sec. 3102]*
Organic Certification	
The Organic Foods Production Act (OFPA) of 1990 (P.L. 101-624, Title XXI; part of the 1990 farm bill), as amended by the 2008 farm bill, authorized the National Organic Program (NOP) to develop and enforce national standards for organically-produced agricultural products. Authorized appropriations were $11 million in FY2012, plus additional sums as necessary. *[7 U.S.C. 6522]*	Reauthorizes appropriations of $15 million annually (FY2013-FY2017). Provides mandatory funding of $5 million in FY2013 (available until expended) to modernize the NOP's database and technology systems. Requires USDA to submit a report to the agriculture committees, within 180 days after enactment, describing, among other things, the feasibility of establishing an organic research and 8 promotion program. *[Section 10005]* Changes effective October 1, 2012. *[Sec. 10011]*
OFPA provides for enforcement and penalties for violations of the program's labeling requirements for certified organic products. *[7 U.S.C. 6519]*	Amends OFPA's recordkeeping, investigations, and enforcement provisions. *[Sec. 10009]* Changes effective October 1, 2012. *[Sec. 10011]*

Current Law/Policy	Senate Agriculture Committee Farm Bill (S. 3240, as filed on May 24, 2012)
See also Title XI (Crop Insurance) for reauthorization of the Organic Certification Cost-Share Program (NOCCSP), established by section 10606 of the 2002 farm bill *[7 U.S.C. 6523]*	*[Sec. 11024]*
Data and Information Collection	
Section 10107 of the 2008 farm bill authorized support for the collection and dissemination of market news for specialty crops. Authorized appropriations $9 million annually (FY2008-FY2012) to remain available until expended. *[7 U.S.C. 1622b(b)]*	Reauthorizes program at $9 million in annual appropriations through FY2017. *[Section 10001]* Changes effective October 1, 2012. *[Sec. 10011]*
Section 7407 of the 2002 farm bill, as amended by the 2008 farm bill, required USDA to keep segregated data on organic production and marketing (Organic Production and Market Data Initiatives, ODI). Provided $5 million in mandatory CCC funding, plus authorized appropriations of $5 million annually (FY2008-FY2012), both available until expended. Specified that $3.5 million of available mandatory funds be allocated to AMS. *[7 U.S.C. 5925c]*	Reauthorizes $5 million in mandatory funding and extends annual appropriations authority of $5 million through FY2017 (available until expended). *[Section 10005]* Changes effective October 1, 2012. *[Sec. 10011]*
No comparable provision.	Requires USDA to collect data on the production and marketing of locally or regionally produced agricultural food products; facilitate interagency collaboration and data sharing on programs related to local and regional food systems; and monitor the effectiveness of programs designed to expand or facilitate local food systems. Requires USDA to submit a report to House and Senate agriculture committees, within 1 year after enactment, describing its progress and identifying any additional needs related to developing local and regional food systems. *[Sec. 10004]* Changes effective October 1, 2012. *[Sec. 10011]*
Pest and Disease Control	
Sections 10201 and 10202 of the 2008 farm bill amended the Plant Protection Act (PPA) to authorize an early plant pest detection and surveillance system and threat identification/mitigation, among other activities, and a National Clean Plant Network where the specialty crop industry can obtain pest- and disease-free planting stock. Provided mandatory CCC funds reaching $50 million in FY2012 (with provisions for annual funding of $50 million annually thereafter), plus another $5 million in FY2008 (available until expended). *[7 U.S.C. 7721]*	Repeals program under section 10202 of the 2008 farm bill and authorizes a consolidated plant pest and disease management and disaster prevention program, named the "National 22 Clean Plant Network". Consolidates and increases available mandatory funding levels: $60 million annually (FY2013-FY2016) and $65 million for FY2017 and each fiscal year thereafter. *[Sec. 10007]* Changes effective October 1, 2012. *[Sec. 10011]*
See also Title VII (Research) for reauthorization of the Office of Pest Management Policy and other pest management policies *[7 U.S.C. 7653]*	See Title VII – Research. *[Sec. 7307]* and *[Sec. 7308]*

Current Law/Policy	Senate Agriculture Committee Farm Bill (S. 3240, as filed on May 24, 2012)
Food Safety and Quality Standards	
Section 10105 of the 2008 farm bill amended the Agricultural Research, Extension, and Education Reform Act of 1998 (P.L. 105-185) to implement a program to educate fresh produce industry personnel and consumers on ways to reduce pathogens in fresh produce. Authorized appropriations of $1 million annually to remain available until expended *[7 U.S.C. 7655a(c)]*	Reauthorizes appropriations of $1 million annually to remain available until expended (FY2013- FY2017). *[Sec. 10006]* Changes effective October 1, 2012. *[Sec. 10011]*
No comparable provision.	Within 180 days after enactment, requires USDA to submit to the Food and Drug Administration (FDA) a report that describes an appropriate federal standard for the identity of honey, and shall consider the March 2006 Standard of Identity citizens petition filed with FDA. *[Sec. 10010]* Changes effective October 1, 2012. *[Sec. 10011]*
Research and Extension (Title VII)	
See also Title VII (Research) for reauthorization of the Specialty Crop Research Initiative (SCRI) *[7 U.S.C. 7632]*, the Organic Agriculture Research and Extension Initiative (OREI) *[7 U.S.C. 5925b]*, the Organic Transitions Program (ORG) *[7 U.S.C. 7626]*, and certain pest management activities *[7 U.S.C. 7653]*	See Title VII – Research. *[Sec. 7305]*, *[Sec. 7208]*, *[Sec. 7302]* and *[Sec. 7102]*
Nutrition (Title IV)	
See also Title IV (Nutrition) for reauthorization of Section 32 funding to purchase fruits, vegetables, and certain other specialty food crops *[7 U.S.C. 612c-4]* and grants to achieve "hunger-free communities", among other related activities *[7 U.S.C. 7517]*	See Title IV – Nutrition. *[Sec. 4201]* and *[Sec. 4205]*

Title XI. Crop Insurance

Current Law/Policy	Senate Agriculture Committee Farm Bill (S. 3240, as filed on May 24, 2012)
New or Revised Insurance Products	
Permanently authorized by the Federal Crop Insurance Act, the federal crop insurance program makes available subsidized crop insurance to producers who purchase a policy to protect against individual farm losses in yield, crop revenue, or whole farm revenue. In general, policies offer a guarantee at the individual farm level or based on area-wide (e.g., county) yields. The producer selects coverage level and absorbs the initial loss through the deductible.	Retains current system and makes available to crop producers an additional policy called **Supplemental Coverage Option (SCO)**, which is a policy based on area-wide (e.g., county) yield or revenue loss. An indemnity would cover all or a part of the deductible under the producer's underlying policy. Coverage cannot exceed 85% of the individual yield or 90% of area yield. Payment occurs only if area loss exceeds 10% of normal level. SCO policies are to be made available for all crops if sufficient data are available. Premium subsidized at 70%. If producer participates in ARC (see Title I), a deductible of 21% applies. Coverage to begin not later than the 2013 crop year. *[Sec. 11001]*
Crop insurance policies are available for more than 100 crops, including farm program crops such as wheat, corn, soybeans, cotton, peanuts, and rice, as well as many specialty crops, fruit trees, pasture, rangeland, and forage crops. Area-wide policies are available for some but not all program crops. Policies are sold and serviced through private insurance companies. The insurance companies' losses are reinsured by USDA, and their administrative and operating costs are reimbursed by the federal government. Crop insurance is administered by the U.S. Department of Agriculture's (USDA's) Risk Management Agency (RMA), which operates and manages the Federal Crop Insurance Corporation (FCIC) *[7 U.S.C. 1501 et seq.]*	Beginning with the 2013 crop, the FCIC shall make available to producers of upland cotton the **Stacked Income Protection Plan (STAX)**, which is a revenue-based, area-wide policy that may be purchased as a stand-alone policy or purchased in addition to any other individual or area policy. Includes a provision that allows use of only recent yields in guarantee. Indemnifies losses in county revenue of greater than 10% of expected revenue but not more than 30%. Premium subsidy is 80%. For individual producers, indemnities for STAX and other policies cannot overlap. *[Sec. 11011]*
	Beginning with the 2013 crop, the FCIC shall make available a **revenue crop insurance program for peanuts** based on a price equal to the Rotterdam price index for peanuts, as adjusted to reflect the farmer stock price of peanuts in the United States. *[Sec. 11012]*
FCIC shall not conduct any pilot program that provides insurance protection against a risk if a policy is generally available from private companies. *[7 U.S.C. 1523(a)]*	FCIC may conduct a pilot program to provide financial assistance for producers of underserved crops and livestock (including specialty crops) to purchase an index-based weather insurance product from a qualified private insurance company. The subsidy shall not exceed 60% of the estimated premium amount. Unlike FCIC policies, the private insurance companies would maintain exclusive rights to rate and manage the policies. Provides mandatory funds of $10 million per year for FY2013 through FY2017. *[Sec. 11021]*
Policy Fees and Premiums	
Catastrophic yield policies (CAT) are available for yield losses greater than 50%. Premium is fully subsidized, and producer pays an administrative fee of $300 per crop per county. *[7 U.S.C. 1508(d)(2)]*	To reduce government costs, the CAT premium (fully paid by government) shall be reduced by the percentage equal to the difference between the average loss ratio (premiums divided by indemnities times 100) for the crop and 100%. *[Sec. 11002]*
Administrative fee on CAT policy is waived for limited resources farmers. *[7 U.S.C. 1508(d)(5)(e)]*	Fee is also waived for beginning farmers or ranchers. *[Sec. 11023]*
Premium subsidies for buy-up coverage (above CAT) depends on level of coverage.	Beginning farmers or ranchers shall receive premium assistance that is 10 percentage points greater than provided to others. Other provisions are also designed to assist beginning farmers and ranchers. *[Sec. 11023]*

Current Law/Policy	Senate Agriculture Committee Farm Bill (S. 3240, as filed on May 24, 2012)
Enterprise Units	
Crops are insured based on geographic units defined in the insurance policy. The basic unit covers land in one county with the same tenant/landlord. An optional unit is a basic unit divided into smaller units by township section. An enterprise unit covers all land of a single crop in a county for a producer, regardless of tenant/landlord structure. A whole farm unit covers more than one crop. For a policy with an enterprise or whole farm unit paragraph, *on a pilot basis*, the percentage of the premium paid by the government shall provide the same dollar amount of premium subsidy per acre as for other units, up to 80%. *[7 U.S.C. 1508(e)(5)]*	The subsidy for enterprise and whole farm units is made permanent (previously a pilot basis). *[Sec. 11003]* Beginning with the 2013 crop year, separate enterprise units will be available for irrigated and nonirrigated acreages of crops. *[Sec. 11004]*
Data Collection for Yield Guarantees; Yield Adjustments	
FCIC bases policy guarantees on a producer's actual production history (APH) for the crop, or on county yields for area-wide policies. The APH is based on producer yields for the prior 4 to 10 years. *[7 U.S.C. 1508(g)(2)]*	Specifically directs FCIC to use county data collected by USDA's Risk Management Agency and/or National Agricultural Statistics Service. If such data are not available, it may use other data considered appropriate by the Secretary of Agriculture. *[Sec. 11005]*
If, for one or more of the crop years used to establish the producer's actual production history of an agricultural commodity, the producer's recorded or appraised yield of the commodity was less than 60% of the applicable transitional yield (based on 10-year historical county average yield), FCIC shall either exclude any of such recorded or appraised yield or replace each excluded yield with a yield equal to 60% of the applicable transitional yield. Concept is known as a "yield plug." *[7 U.S.C. 1508(g)(4)(B)]*	Beginning with the 2013 crop year, the yield plug is increased to 70% of the applicable transitional yield. *[Sec. 11006]*
Policy Research Development, Review, and Approval	
Under sections 522 and 523 of the Federal Crop Insurance Act, FCIC may enter into contracts to carry out research and development for new crop insurance policies (but may not conduct research itself). It shall provide a payment to an applicant for research and development costs. FCIC may approve up to 50% of the projected total research and development costs to be paid in advance to an applicant. *[7 U.S.C. 1522]*	Allows FCIC to conduct research and development activities to maintain or improve existing policies or develop new policies. *[Sec. 11019]* FCIC shall review any policy developed under section 522(c)or any pilot program developed under section 523 and submit the policy or program to the Board if it finds that the policy or program will likely result in a viable and marketable policy and would provide coverage in a significantly improved form. *[Sec. 11007]* For cost reimbursement, the 50% limitation may be waived and, upon request of the submitter, an additional 25% advance payment may be made. *[Sec. 11015]*

Current Law/Policy	Senate Agriculture Committee Farm Bill (S. 3240, as filed on May 24, 2012)
Adjusted Gross Revenue (AGR) and AGR-Lite policies insure revenue of the entire farm rather than an individual crop. Both use a producer's five-year historical farm average revenue as reported on the Internal Revenue Service (IRS) tax return form (Schedule F or equivalent forms). Coverage levels range from 65% to 80% of historical revenue. *[7 U.S.C. 1523]*	FCIC is to conduct activities or enter into contracts to develop a **whole farm risk management insurance plan** (with liability up to $1.5 million) that pays an indemnity if gross farm revenue is below 85% (compared with 80% currently). Coverage may include value of packing, packaging or other on-farm activities. FCIC may provide diversification-based discounts for producers with diversified operations. *[Sec. 11016]*
	FCIC is required to contract with a qualified person to conduct a study to determine the feasibility of insuring swine producers for a catastrophic disease event and submit a report to Congress. *[Sec. 11017]* FCIC is also required to study the feasibility of insuring producers of fresh-water catfish against reduction in the margin between the market value of catfish and selected production costs. The FCIC Board shall review this policy and approve it under certain conditions. *[Sec. 11018]*
A private sector entity can propose an insurance plan to be added to the FCIC portfolio of products. A process must be established to review and approve products. *[7 U.S.C. 1508(h)]*	For private sector submissions, adds similar language found in Section 11007 plus directs FCIC to establish priorities for specific types of submissions. *[Section 11008]* As part of the submission process, the applicant must consult with producer groups potentially affected. *[Sec. 11009]*
FCIC may conduct a pilot program approved by the Board to evaluate whether a proposal or new risk management tool is suitable for the marketplace and addresses the needs of producers. *[7 U.S.C. 1523(a)]*	Eliminates the requirement that FCIC evaluate pilot programs and submit a report to Congress. *[Sec. 11020]*
Crop Production on Native Sod	
Native sod planted to an insurable crop (over 5 acres) is ineligible for crop insurance and the noninsured crop disaster assistance program for the first 5 years of planting. May apply to virgin prairie converted to cropland in the Prairie Pothole National Priority Area, if elected by the state. *[7 U.S.C. 1508(o)]*	Nationwide, on land that has never been tilled, crop insurance premium subsidies are 50 percentage points less than under current schedule during the first 4 years of planting. Also, no benefits are available under the Noninsured Crop Disaster or general commodity programs. Requires annual reports on the change in cropland areas in each county and state. *[Sec. 11025]*
Standard Reinsurance Agreement and Risk-Sharing	
The Standard Reinsurance Agreement (SRA) between FCIC and private companies defines expense reimbursements and risk-sharing by the government, including the terms under which the government provides subsidies and reinsurance (i.e., insurance for insurance companies) on eligible crop insurance contracts sold or reinsured by insurance companies. FCIC may renegotiate the SRA once every 5 years. *[7 U.S.C. 1508(k)]*	Any savings generated from a renegotiated SRA must be used for programs administered by the Risk Management Agency. *[Sec. 11010]*
Miscellaneous	
Inaccurate information on an insurance application can result in noncompliance, which voids the policy and may disqualify the producer for up to 5 years *[7 U.S.C. 1515(c)]*	FCIC shall establish procedures that allow an agent and approved insurance provider to correct information regarding producer name and eligibility information that is provided by a producer for the purpose of obtaining coverage. *[Sec. 11013]*

Current Law/Policy	Senate Agriculture Committee Farm Bill (S. 3240, as filed on May 24, 2012)
USDA is to ensure that new hardware and software for administering the program are compatible with that already used by USDA agencies in order to maximize data sharing needed for proper program delivery. *[7 U.S.C. 1515(j)]* Funding is provided from the insurance fund: $15 million for each of FY2008 through FY2010 and not more than $9 million in FY2011. *[7 U.S.C. 1515(k)]*	The Secretary shall develop and implement an acreage report streamlining initiative project to allow producers to report acreage and other information directly to USDA. FCIC may use up to $25 million in fiscal 2013 and $10 to $15 million per year for FY2014 through FY2017 from the insurance fund. USDA shall notify Congress on the status of the project no later than July 13, 2013. *[Sec. 11014]*
The Agricultural Management Assistance Program provides financial assistance to producers in 16 specific states to mitigate risk through financial instruments, diversification, or resource conservation practices. Provides $15 million in annual mandatory funding in FY2008 through FY2014, and $10 million each fiscal year thereafter. Requires 50% for conservation, 40% for risk management, and 10% for organic certification. *[7 U.S.C. 1524]* Section 10606 of the 2002 farm bill established a National Organic Certification Cost-Share Program to help producers and handlers of organic products obtain certification. Provided $22 million in mandatory funding in FY2008 (available until expended). *[7 U.S.C. 6523]*	Authorizes $23 million in mandatory CCC funding annually (FY2013-FY2017) and combines the two programs to include: (1) organic certification cost share assistance (50% of funds); (2) activities to support risk management education and outreach under the Federal Crop Insurance Act (26% of funds); and (3) agricultural management assistance grants to producers in states with low federal crop insurance participation, for various conservation purposes (24% of funds). Per-person payments are limited to $50,000 in any one year. *[Sec. 11024]*

Title XII. Miscellaneous

Current Law/Policy	Senate Agriculture Committee Farm Bill (S. 3240, as filed on May 24, 2012)
Subtitle A: Socially Disadvantage Producers and Limited Resource Producers	
Outreach and Assistance for Socially Disadvantaged Farmers and Ranchers. Outreach and Assistance for Socially Disadvantaged Farmers and Ranchers was established by Sec. 2501 of the 1990 farm bill. The program provides education and outreach to minority and limited-resource farmers and ranchers. The 2008 farm bill created an Office of Small Farms and Beginning Farmers and Ranchers to ensure access to all USDA programs for small, beginning, and socially disadvantaged farmers and ranchers. Also requires USDA to document the number, location, and economic contributions of socially disadvantaged and limited-resource farmers and ranchers. Provides the program with $15 million in mandatory funding annually through FY2012. *[7 U.S.C. 2279(a)]*	Expands program authority to include farmers and ranchers who are veterans. Authorizes $20 million annually, subject to annual appropriations for FY2013-FY2017. *[Sec. 12001]*
Office of Advocacy and Outreach. The Office of Advocacy and Outreach as authorized in the 2008 farm bill carries out the Outreach and Assistance for Socially Disadvantaged Farmers and Ranchers and Veteran Farmers and Ranchers, and also oversees the Minority Farmer Advisory Committee and carries out the functions of the Office of Outreach and Diversity previously handled by the Office of Assistant Secretary for Civil Rights. *[7 U.S.C. 6934(f)(3)]*	For the Office of Advocacy and Outreach, authorizes such sums as necessary for FY2009 through FY2012, and $2 million annually for FY2013-FY2017, subject to annual appropriations. *[Sec. 12002]*
Subtitle B: Livestock	
Wildlife Reservoir Zoonotic Disease Initiative. No comparable provision. Amends Title IV of the Agricultural Research, Extension, and Education Reform Act of 1998. *[7 U.S.C. 7621 et seq.]*	Establishes an initiative through competitive grants for research and development of surveillance methods, vaccinations, vaccination delivery systems, or diagnostic tests. The targeted diseases are brucellosis, bovine tuberculosis, and other high priority disease initiatives conducted under Sec. 1672 of the Food, Agriculture, Conservation, and Trade Act of 1990 *[7 U.S.C. 5925]*. The research may be conducted by federal agencies, national laboratories, universities, research institutes, and state agricultural experiment stations. The grants are not to exceed 10 years and require matching funds of at least 25% of the federal contribution. $7 million per year is authorized to be appropriated FY2012-FY2017. *[Sec. 12101]*
Trichinae Certification Program. Sec. 11010 of the 2008 farm bill established a voluntary trichinae certification program. *[7 U.S.C. §8304 note]* The program certifies compliance with best production practices and is designed to enhance swine and pork producers' ability to export fresh pork and pork products. Authorizes appropriation of $1.5 million for Sec. 11010 and funds as necessary to carry out Sec. 10405 of the Animal Health Protection Act (AHPA) for FY2008 through FY2012. *[7 U.S.C. 8304(d)(1)]*	Reauthorizes current level of $1.5 million each year through FY2017, subject to annual appropriations. *[Sec. 12102]*

Current Law/Policy	Senate Agriculture Committee Farm Bill (S. 3240, as filed on May 24, 2012)
National Aquatic Animal Health Plan. Sec. 11013 of the 2008 farm bill authorized USDA, under Sec. 10411 of the AHPA, *[7 U.S.C. 8310]* to enter into cooperative agreements for the purpose of detecting, controlling, or eradicating diseases of aquaculture species and promoting species-specific best management practices on a cost-share basis. Secretary may use authorities from AHPA *[7 U.S.C. 8301 et seq.]* to carry out the plan. Authorizes such sums as necessary to be appropriated in each fiscal year, FY2008-FY2012. *[7 U.S.C. 8322]*	Extends funding authority for the plan through FY2017. *[Sec. 12103]*
Sheep Production and Marketing Grant Program.	Establishes a competitive grant program through USDA's Agricultural Marketing Service to improve the sheep industry, including infrastructure, business, resource development, or
No comparable provision.	innovative approaches for long-term needs. $1.5 million in CCC mandatory funds for FY2013 to be used and remain available until expended. *[Sec. 12104]*
The National Sheep Industry Improvement Center (NSIIC) promotes the strategic development of the U.S. sheep and goat industry. It provides financial assistance for the enhancement and marketing of sheep and goat products with an emphasis on infrastructure development. NSIIC is funded through appropriations, as well as receipts from products or services, fees and royalties from licensing, proceeds from sales of assets, loan or equity interest, and donations. *[7 U.S.C. 2008(j)]*	Amends provisions of the NSIIC. Amends the percentage of funds from 3% to 10% that may be used for administration of the NSIIC, and removes the authorization of appropriations. Re-designates the NSIIC from the Consolidated Farm and Rural Development Act [7 U.S.C. 2008(j)] to the Agricultural Marketing Act of 1946 [7 U.S.C. 1621 et seq.]. *[Sec. 12104]*
Feral Swine Eradication Pilot Program. No comparable provision.	Establishes pilot program to study the (1) nature and extent of damage caused by feral swine; (2) methods to eradicate or control feral swine; and (3) methods to restore damage caused by feral swine. USDA's Natural Resources Conservation Service and Animal and Plant Health Inspection Service are to coordinate on the program. The program is to be administered on a cost-sharing basis with the federal share not to exceed 75%. The non-federal share may be in-kind contribution. $2 million per year is authorized to be appropriated for FY2013-2017. *[Sec. 12105]*
Subtitle C: Other Miscellaneous Provisions	
Military Veterans Agricultural Liaison. No comparable provision.	Amends Subtitle A of the Department of Agriculture Reorganization Act of 1994 [7 U.S.C. 6901 et seq] by establishing in USDA a position of Military Veterans Agricultural Liaison to provide information to returning veterans on beginning farmer training, agricultural vocational and rehabilitation programs. Liaison would provide information on availability and eligibility for participation, serve as a resource, and advocate on behalf of veterans within USDA. *[Sec. 12201]*

Current Law/Policy	Senate Agriculture Committee Farm Bill (S. 3240, as filed on May 24, 2012)
Information Gathering. USDA may not disclose information about an agricultural operation, farming or conservation practice, or land that was provided by the producer or landowner in order to qualify for a USDA program, nor the geospatial information maintained by USDA about the agricultural land or operations mentioned above. Exceptions are provided for the limited release of data to federal, state, local or tribal agencies working in cooperation with USDA when providing technical or financial assistance for the above land or when responding to pest and disease threats. However, USDA must determine that the data will not be subsequently disclosed. The prohibition on data disclosure does not affect the release of payment information that is otherwise authorized or data that is released in an aggregate, personally unidentifiable form. *[7 U.S.C. 8791; also known as Section 1619 of the 2008 farm bill]*	Adds language to clarify and strengthen the conditions necessary to release data about farms to state and local government agencies. Such state and other government agencies would need to prove that the data are "required for implementing" the state program. Moreover, the data may only be used by the state agency, political subdivision, or local agency; and the data would be protected from subsequent disclosure by the state or agency. *[Sec. 12202]*
Grants to Improve Supply, Stability, Safety, and Training of Agricultural Labor Force. Provides grants to train farm workers in new technologies and workers with specialized skills for higher value crops. Authorized funds to be appropriated as necessary for FY2008-FY2012. *[7 U.S.C. 2008q-1(d)]*	Grant program extended. $10 million per year authorized to be appropriated for FY2013-FY2017. *[Sec. 12203]*
Noninsured Crop Assistance Program. The Noninsured Crop Assistance Program (NAP) has permanent authority under Section 196 of the Federal Agriculture Improvement and Reform Act of 1996, and receives such sums as necessary in mandatory funding. Growers of crops not insurable under the crop insurance program are eligible for NAP. A payment is made to an eligible producer whose actual production is less than 50% of the established (historical) yield for the crop. The payment rate is 55% of the average market price. Producers pay a fee of $250 per crop per county, or $750 per producer per county, not to exceed $1,875 per producer. *[7 USC 7333]*	Through FY2017, makes available additional coverage for NAP at 50% to 65% of established yield and 100% of average market price. Premium for additional coverage is 5.25% times the product of the selected coverage level and value of production (acreage times yield times average market price). The premium for additional coverage is reduced by 50% for limited resource, beginning, and socially disadvantaged farmers. Eliminates NAP for crops/grasses used for grazing (to reduce overlap with livestock disaster programs in Title I—Commodity Programs), ferns, and tropical fish. Increases base NAP fee to $260 per crop per county, or $780 per producer per county, not to exceed $1,950 per producer. *[Sec. 12204]*
Regional Economic and Infrastructure Development. The 2008 farm bill (Section 14217) established three new regional development authorities: a Northern Border Regional Commission, a Southeast Crescent Regional Commission, and a Southwest Border Regional Commission. These commissions develop a regional development plan and then make infrastructure loans and grants to eligible entities in their respective regions. *[40 U.S.C. 15101 et seq.]* Authorizes annual appropriations of $30 million to each of the Commissions. Not more than 10% of appropriated funds to any Commission can be used for administrative expenses. *[40 U.S.C. 15751(b)]*	Allows the cap on administrative expense for any Commission to exceed 10% should the Commission receive an annual appropriation of less then $10 million. *[Sec. 12205]*

Current Law/Policy	Senate Agriculture Committee Farm Bill (S. 3240, as filed on May 24, 2012)
Canada Geese Removal. No comparable provision.	If the Federal Aviation Administration determines that a population of Canada geese residing on National Park Service land within 5 miles of any commercial airport poses a risk to air traffic, USDA, through its Animal and Plant Health Inspection Service, will publish a management plan by the first molting season following enactment. The plan must provide for the removal of geese on all applicable land within one year of its publication. Also, by June 1, 2012, USDA is to issue a decision on a plan for removing geese from National Park Service land near JFK International Airport in New York. This removal is to be completed by August 1, 2012. *[Sec. 12206]*

Author Contact Information

Ralph M. Chite, Coordinator
Section Research Manager
rchite@crs.loc.gov, 7-7296

Dennis A. Shields
Specialist in Agricultural Policy
dshields@crs.loc.gov, 7-9051

Megan Stubbs
Analyst in Agricultural Conservation and Natural
Resources Policy
mstubbs@crs.loc.gov, 7-8707

Charles E. Hanrahan
Senior Specialist in Agricultural Policy
chanrahan@crs.loc.gov, 7-7235

Randy Alison Aussenberg
Analyst in Nutrition Assistance Policy
raussenberg@crs.loc.gov, 7-8641

Jim Monke
Specialist in Agricultural Policy
jmonke@crs.loc.gov, 7-9664

Tadlock Cowan
Analyst in Natural Resources and Rural
Development
tcowan@crs.loc.gov, 7-7600

Randy Schnepf
Specialist in Agricultural Policy
rschnepf@crs.loc.gov, 7-4277

Renée Johnson
Specialist in Agricultural Policy
rjohnson@crs.loc.gov, 7-9588

Joel L. Greene
Analyst in Agricultural Policy
jgreene@crs.loc.gov, 7-9877

Remy Jurenas
Specialist in Agricultural Policy
rjurenas@crs.loc.gov, 7-7281

Acknowledgments

Special thanks to CRS editor Laura Comay for her technical assistance in publishing this report.